# LIVING ALONE

### INFORMATION FOR MEN WHO FIND THEMSELVES ON THEIR OWN.

### PETER MULRANEY

Copyright © 2015 Peter Mulraney

All rights reserved.

No part of this book may be reproduced in any form or by any electronic or mechanical means, including information storage and retrieval systems, without written permission from the author, except for the use of brief quotations in a book review.

ISBN: 978-0-6482523-3-7

This edition published 2018.

❀ Created with Vellum

# CONTENTS

*Preface*     v

## AFTER SHE'S GONE

| | |
|---|---|
| Introduction | 3 |
| Process the ending | 5 |
| It's your place now | 9 |
| Keeping the place clean | 11 |
| The mysteries of the laundry | 18 |
| Outsourcing | 22 |
| Money management | 24 |

## COOKING 4 ONE

| | |
|---|---|
| Introduction | 31 |
| Some basic stuff | 33 |
| Preparing meals | 42 |
| Breakfast | 46 |
| Lunch | 56 |
| Dinner | 61 |
| Sample menus | 81 |
| Entertaining | 85 |
| Over to you | 88 |

## SANITY SAVERS

| | |
|---|---|
| Introduction | 93 |
| Reading | 95 |
| Writing | 102 |
| Learning a new skill | 108 |
| Exercising | 114 |
| Growing things | 122 |
| Serving | 126 |

| | |
|---|---|
| Having fun | 130 |
| Staying connected | 135 |
| Befriending yourself | 142 |
| Summary | 149 |
| | |
| *A note from Peter* | 151 |
| *Also by Peter Mulraney* | 153 |

# PREFACE

For those of us in middle or old age, finding ourselves living alone after the end of a long-term relationship can be a bit of a challenge. Not only is there all the emotional stuff to deal with, there is also the need to start looking after ourselves, sometimes for the first time in our lives.

When the woman in your life has gone, for whatever reason, all those things she did in the kitchen and around the house are suddenly no longer secret women's business. Now they're your business; and your health and well-being depend on how well you master them. Most of us can't afford the luxury of outsourcing all or any of it, so we have to learn to do it for ourselves.

It's easy to be discouraged when you first try and work out how things work in the kitchen, especially if you've never done any cooking or food shopping. It's tempting to take the easy way out and live on takeaways. From my perspective, it's best not to go down that street.

*Preface*

Keep in mind that if you can boil a saucepan of water on a stove or cooktop, there are a lot of things you can drop into that boiling water and turn into a meal in minutes. I share some of the ways I use a saucepan of boiling water in the section: Cooking 4 One.

When you're doing the cleaning, remember, if it appears to be overwhelming you can always chunk it. If chunking works for project management, it will work for cleaning a house or an apartment - just do a bit at a time. That's how I do it. I break the cleaning down into manageable tasks and do them regularly. You don't have to fall in love with cleaning and keeping things in some sort of order - you simply have to do it.

I don't know anybody who loves ironing. I know I don't, and I know how to do it. My best advice is to buy shirts that don't need ironing if you can, and remember to let then dry on a hanger. Stay away from any idea that you have to iron sheets and pillowcases, or tea towels and tablecloths for that matter. If you're stuck with cotton or linen tablecloths, do yourself a favour and buy something that doesn't need ironing or use place mats.

Apart from looking after yourself physically, you need to look after yourself mentally and emotionally.

In the Sanity Savers section I share nine strategies for finding constructive ways to fill in your time and maintain your sanity. You don't have to embrace them all but I do encourage you to stay connected and to befriend yourself.

A lot of us put off doing the personal growth stuff, because we're afraid of what we'll find if we start looking 'under the hood'. I can only tell you that it's therapeutic - it's good for you - if you're prepared to spend some time doing it.

In the end, life is what you make it, so be kind to yourself and enjoy this new way of being.

## Preface

The content of *Living Alone* is taken from the three titles in the Living Alone series: *After She's Gone, Cooking4One* and *Sanity Savers*. Although those names appear as section headings, the content of each section has been edited to remove duplication and consolidate material for the purposes of clarity.

# AFTER SHE'S GONE

# INTRODUCTION

Sometimes it feels like life happens to you, especially when your journey intersects with death, divorce or desertion; or you find yourself temporarily separated from the woman who had been taking care of business at your place.

It happened to me. Around five years ago, my wife, who had been looking after me in Adelaide, Australia, for thirty something years at that point, decided she wanted to broaden her horizons by becoming an educational consultant in New York. Yeah, you got it, the one in the United States of America. That's a tad more than a cut lunch and a water bottle trip from my place - by 747.

For reasons associated with financial commitments and maximizing my retirement savings plan, I chose to stay at my job in Australia.

No need to feel sorry, it's working out fine. We're still married and we get to spend time together in two different cities, in two different parts of the world, in two different time zones, and I found out about Skype.

*Introduction*

But, I found myself living on my own again, for up to four or five months at a time.

There's only so much stuff a woman can leave behind in the freezer, and if she's left for good, she may not have left you anything in the freezer, and she's certainly not going to be on Skype, telling you how to cook whatever it is you want to try this week.

In a way, I was lucky. Being a country boy, I'd had some experience looking after myself when I was at university. We country kids had to leave home and come down to the city to study, and I ended up living in an apartment with a couple of my brothers. So, I had some basic cooking skills I could fall back on. And, having been one of those collaborative husbands, who shared the housework while we were raising our kids, I knew how things about the house worked.

My wife would say that I was well trained. I might not have mastered much in the kitchen, but at least I'd done some sort of an apprenticeship over the years. I might not make the bed the way she wants it made, but at least I know how to make a bed, and I've done enough supervised cleaning to know which end of the vacuum cleaner is the business end.

Having looked after myself successfully for a while, I thought it might be useful to share what I know, so that anyone finding himself in a similar situation, would have access to a basic survival guide written by a fellow traveller, one who had survived by acquiring the basic skills required to look after himself.

*Disclaimer:* I'm no expert. I'm simply a practitioner, who has relied on the ideas discussed in this section and lived to tell you about them.

# PROCESS THE ENDING

Before we move on to the skills you need to master to look after yourself, let's take a moment to consider processing the end of your relationship.

The macho thing is to tough it out, to pretend it doesn't hurt and soldier on. That might work on the battlefield in the short-term heat of the fight. Anywhere else in life it's bullshit.

All relationship endings, whether through death or divorce, involve emotional pain you need to deal with. Grieving is the name we give to that process.

## Grieving

The end of any relationship is painful. Most of us think of grieving only in terms of death, but grieving is simply a process of working through a sense of loss.

I'm not a grief counsellor, but I've had some experience with grieving:

- people in my life have died,
- relationships have ended before I was ready, and
- friends have moved away to different parts of the world

- and you probably have too.

No matter how your relationship ended, it's important for your mental and emotional well-being to grieve appropriately.

A useful resource, that will not cost you the earth, is *Good Grief 50^(th) Anniversary Edition* by Granger E Westberg, which you can buy on Amazon. If you don't feel like buying the book you can ask our friend Google about the grieving process - he's got lots of resources you can read for free.

One thing you should be aware of is that grieving is not done well with alcohol - or any other mind numbing drug for that matter.

Another is, it's okay for a grown man to cry.

Something else I've learnt about grieving is that it's good to have someone to talk it through with, someone who will just listen - without judging or telling you to pull yourself together and get over her.

Give yourself the time and space to grieve. Trying to pretend it doesn't hurt doesn't work. You might think you can fool yourself, and everybody else, into believing that you're okay, that you're over her, but unless you've done the processing that grief will surface later, when you least expect it.

So do yourself a favour - be honest with yourself about how you feel.

## Legals

At the end of any long-term relationship there will be a few loose ends.

If you're dealing with moving on from the death of your spouse or partner, there will be a pile of legal stuff to deal with to finalize her estate.

The level of detail required to finalize an estate depends on the country you live in, and the number and type of assets involved. Some things have dollar amount thresholds and timeframes attached to them. In some countries you have to pay death or estate taxes, so go online and find out what the tax obligations are in your country.

Hopefully, if she had a lot of assets, she left a will with instructions for how her things are to be distributed. If her estate is complicated, get help. That's why we have lawyers and accountants.

If you're moving on from a divorce, follow through with whatever you agreed to with your ex or with what the court imposed. That way you'll avoid any unnecessary fees from her team. If you need to get things transferred into or out of your name or hers, get it done. Now that you are no longer a couple, you don't want to continue any joint and several liabilities you undertook as a couple either.

If you're getting over the end of a long-term non-matrimonial or de facto relationship, you might still need some legal advice, especially if you live in a country like Australia where, from a legal perspective, a de facto relationship is treated the same as a marriage.

If your split is not amicable and you have lots of assets, don't put off speaking to your lawyer or accountant.

You can ask our friend Google but, in the end, you'll be better served by talking to a lawyer and a tax accountant if you need advice.

My advice is don't put it off.

**Her stuff**

If you're moving on from the death of a spouse or partner, at some point you need to do something with her personal items, like clothing and jewellery.

This can be pretty hard emotionally, so if you have children, you might want to consider asking them to help you.

Stuff that you can't use can be given a new life with someone else. Some stuff you have to throw out. Your children might want some items, like her favourite pieces of jewellery.

There are lots of organisations, like the St Vincent de Paul Society or the Salvation Army, that can make good use of clothing and other items. Give them a call. Some of them collect, others will ask you to bring things in or drop them off at a specific location.

If she was a journal writer, you might be faced with the dilemma I gave one of the characters in my novel *After*. If you read her journals you could find out some things you'd rather not know. A tough choice, but if you ever want to write the story of her life, don't throw them out. Perhaps you can share them with your children or save them to pass on at your death.

Remember, when you clear out the old you're making room for the new.

# IT'S YOUR PLACE NOW

I don't know about you, but I don't know too many guys living with a wife or girlfriend, who have the ultimate say in interior decorating. So, if you have recently come out of a long-term relationship with a woman, chances are a lot of things in your living space will still be arranged in accordance with her preferences - unless you're the one who moved out.

## Making it yours

Now that you're living on your own, you get to arrange things to suit yourself. Everything: from the way things are arranged in the drawers in the kitchen, to the shelves in the pantry and the fridge, to the furniture in the living room. You get all the space in the vanity in the bathroom and you can do what you like with the toothpaste.

If you don't like the girly duvet cover on the bed, go buy yourself something you do like. If you don't want those doily things she had all over the place, put them away or chuck them out.

Now that the default position is you being in charge, you can leave the toilet seat up, put your beer in the fridge in the kitchen or your wine in the pantry, if you want to. If you prefer to cook on the BBQ, that's your call. If you want to watch the TV news while you're eating your evening meal, you can. If you want to sleep in on weekends, go ahead. If you want to spend Saturday or Sunday afternoon with your favourite paper and a glass of red, it's your call.

Relax - there is no-one criticising the way you make the bed, wash the dishes or drop water on the floor, unless you're into talking to yourself.

The downside is there is no-one else to do any of the things that need to be done around the place. That's all up to you now - but you get to do them in your own time.

When it's your place you get to set the acceptable standard and to live with the consequences - so be good to yourself.

# KEEPING THE PLACE CLEAN

You may be the only one living in the house or apartment now but it will still need cleaning. It may be a mystery where all that dust comes from but it still comes. The other thing about cleaning up after yourself is maintaining order or keeping the place tidy.

Take my word for it, it doesn't take long for chaos to establish itself if you neglect to keep on top of the maintaining order bit, and it's a lot more work getting chaos out of the house than it is in refusing to let it sneak in.

There are two approaches to cleaning and maintaining order that I find helpful: the 'as you go along method' and the 'regular routine'. In other words, there are some things you can do daily and there are others you will want to do weekly or less frequently.

### General cleaning tasks

Let's start by considering a few general cleaning tasks, before we focus on some specific rooms.

## Air conditioner

If you have an air conditioner with a filter, remember to clean the filter on a regular basis. The easiest way is with water. If you have a yard, take it out and use the hose on it. If it fits into your laundry trough or bath, give it a soak and then shake it out, dry it off and return it to the air conditioner.

If in doubt - read the manual.

If you can't find the manual, go visit your friend Google and ask him to find it for you.

## Flat surfaces

Thanks to gentle breezes and gravity, flat surfaces, including furniture, the top of the fridge, the cover or hood of the exhaust fan, exposed shelves and the seats of chairs, collect dust. You need to wipe them with a cloth, and remember to apply some furniture polish to wooden furniture every now and then.

## Floors

If your place has carpet on the floors, you need to master the vacuum cleaner, and set up a weekly routine for high traffic areas, and maybe a monthly routine for other parts of the house that don't get much use. The thing to remember about vacuum cleaners is that they need to be emptied and maintained. If you can't find the manual, go visit your friend Google and ask him for a copy.

If you have other floor coverings, like tiles or floorboards, you'll need to locate the broom and the mop. Sweep the floors weekly and give them a once over with a wet mop, at least once a month. You might want to make that weekly in the kitchen and bathroom. Note: a wet mop usually requires some sort of bucket, and unless you're particularly messy, you only need to use water with a wet mop. The idea is to remove dust from the floor, not sterilize it - you don't have to eat off it!

## Mirrors

Another surface to watch out for is any mirror in the house. Somehow, even though they're vertical, they still attract dust. A mirror takes a bit more work. Use a glass cleaning spray and a soft cloth.

## Rooms

There are some rooms in a house or apartment that you use more frequently than others, and some of these require specific attention.

## Bathroom

The bathroom is one room that requires constant vigilance, simply because it's where you splash water about and steam the place up.

Two things I find helpful: ditching the soap and using a shower gel makes it a lot easier to keep the shower clean, and staying on top of the mould that loves to grow in the grout between tiles or the silicon sealant that helps keep the water in the bathroom. I tried a lot of products in my effort to kill the mould in my shower, and finally settled on Selleys Rapid Mould Killer, because it worked.

No matter which approach you take, you'll need to wipe down the tiles with a wet cloth, after you have sprayed on some cleaning product to loosen the hold of the soap or gel residue. Glass shower screens respond to glass cleaner, and if you're using a shower curtain, give it a regular wash in the washing machine.

If you have an exhaust fan in your bathroom, its filter will get clogged with fluff from towels over time. One easy way to clean it is with the vacuum cleaner.

Vacuum the floor, and inside the bath, on a regular basis to suck up all those hairs, bits of fluff and talcum powder that gather there, and mop the floor regularly, so that you aren't tracking that stuff all over the house.

Toilet training - if you're regular it's not a big job.

Invest in a brush and use it every time you make a deposit. Install an automatic toilet cleaner that operates every time you flush. Remember to wipe down the outside of the bowl, the seat (spray on disinfectant) and the lid, and if you drip on the floor, clean it up before you flush - it's a lot easier than scrubbing off the dried version later, and you won't be embarrassed when guests use your loo.

If your toilet is in a separate room, remember to vacuum and mop the floor when you're cleaning the bathroom.

## Bedroom

This is one room where fluff and lint from clothing and bed clothes accumulate on the floor, so regular treatment with the vacuum cleaner is essential. The other thing to watch for is dust on the flat surfaces of your bedroom furniture.

Just because you're living on your own, it's not a good idea to revert to adolescent behaviour when it comes to clothes. Get a laundry basket to dump your dirty clothes into, instead of dropping them on the floor, and hang your clothes up in the wardrobe. Being organised with your clothes makes it easier to find them, and avoids that crumpled look that you then have to correct with ironing.

The main item in the bedroom is the bed. Whether you make it or not is a personal choice. It looks better if it's made but an unmade bed 'sleeps' just as well as a made one. The thing to remember is to change the bedding regularly.

If you use both a top and bottom sheet, the duvet cover and the mattress protector only need washing every now and then, but the sheets and pillow cases should be washed more frequently, like weekly - especially if you don't wear pyjamas.

## Kitchen

The kitchen is one place where you need to apply the 'as you go method'.

Cooking can create a mess, and sometimes those messes can be spectacular, especially if you get distracted and things boil over on the cooktop or stove, or the lid flies off a dish in the microwave oven.

Wipe down the inside of the microwave oven after any spills. Remember to do the inside of the door. The rotating glass plate comes out for easy cleaning.

If you make a mess on the stove, clean it up as soon as practicable. You don't want to burn yourself for the sake of cleanliness, so sometimes you need to let things cool down before you can clean them up. But, be warned: the longer you leave it the harder it will be to remove.

If you have an exhaust or extractor fan there's more to cleaning it than the hood. The filters that trap oils and particles released during cooking need regular cleaning as well. Soak them in hot water and detergent, give them a rinse and dry them out before you use them again. One way to dry them is to put them back in and run the exhaust fan.

One area that needs constant cleaning is the bench top you use to cut things up on, even if you use a cutting board. And, that cutting board needs to be cleaned every time you use it. Another is the sink. A sink can be a bacteria trap, so rinse it out and give it a regular clean with Ajax powder cleaner or something similar.

That dishcloth you use for cleaning things up with on the bench and washing dishes in the sink - give it a rinse every time you use it and hang it up, so it gets a chance to dry between uses, and either wash it (in the washing machine) or chuck it out at least once a week.

Another thing that it pays to attend to daily is washing up the pots and pans and dishes associated with cooking and eating. If you have a dishwasher, load it up and use it after dinner. If you prefer to wash your dishes by hand, do it after each meal. That way it never becomes overwhelming.

Modern fridges and freezers auto-defrost, and although you don't have to shut them down and scrape out the ice anymore, you still need to keep the interior, especially of the fridge, clean. Again, cleaning up spills as you make them is best, and you can take preventive measures, like thawing out a ziplock bag of meat inside a bowl.

If you're stuck with an older model freezer that needs to be defrosted, use a cooler or an esky with some ice packs to hold the contents of the freezer while you defrost it. And remember, no sharp instruments for the defrosting, or you'll be shopping for a new freezer sooner than you had planned.

**Living room**

Unless the kitchen is the focal point of your house, you probably spend a lot of time in this room, reading, watching TV and entertaining visitors, so it's probably a good idea to keep it clean and tidy with a weekly once over with the vacuum cleaner. Remember those flat surfaces and don't forget the armchairs.

# THE MYSTERIES OF THE LAUNDRY

Not only are you now responsible for keeping the house clean, you also need to do something about keeping your clothes clean too.

This is where doing the laundry comes in. If you've never actually managed this process before it might seem a little mysterious but all it requires is a bit of planning.

**Washing and drying clothes**

My recommendation is that you do it weekly, otherwise it can become a real chore.

The modern laundry, with a washing machine and a clothes dryer, allows you to wash and dry clothes regardless of the weather. In addition to a clothes dryer, I suggest you invest in a drying rack and, when the weather allows, you use the solar powered clothes line in the yard, if you have one.

Washing works best if you separate your dirty stuff into piles before you start. The following sort works for me:

- shirts,
- underwear, tee-shirts and socks,
- sheets and pillow cases,
- towels, tea towels and dish clothes,
- jeans, trousers and shorts, and
- woollen jumpers.

Most weeks I only have four piles. You could combine some of the piles but you risk getting fluff from your socks all over your shirts or from your towels all over your sheets.

The other secret is to wash using cold water and a washing powder or liquid that works in cold water. Colors don't bleed or run in cold water. The only other product I use is fabric softener with the towels.

Unless you get your clothes really dirty, select the quick wash cycle, load your pile into the machine, add the powder or liquid into the dispenser, make sure the door is closed, and turn on the power and the water.

I never put the shirts into the dryer. I hang them on hangers, either on the outside line or a drying rack. This approach, combined with choosing polyester and cotton shirts, means I don't have to iron my shirts. To be honest, I do have a few cotton shirts that need ironing, but they get less wrinkled drying this way, which makes them easier to iron.

When the weather is against me, I have no problem throwing the sheets and towels in the dryer but I use the drying rack for everything else.

If you wash a woollen jumper, lay it flat on a towel on a table, or roll it up inside a towel, to draw the water out for a few hours before hanging it on the drying rack.

When the washing is dry, fold it up and put it away. That way you'll know where your clothes are when you want to wear them.

Like all machines, a washing machine requires some not so obvious basic maintenance. The washing supplies dispenser needs to be cleaned on a regular basis to prevent the growth of mould and blockages. If the dispenser comes out, remove it and give it a good wash every couple of months. If your machine has a drain hole, open it every couple of months to remove any build up of material. If it's a front loader, wipe out the inside of the sealing rubber around the drum, and leave the door open each week after you use it. If you don't, you will soon find out why you should.

**Ironing**

There are ways to avoid it, but if you have to do it all it takes is practice and patience. If you have no idea about how to do it, visit your friend Google and ask him about ironing a shirt. He's got some very helpful videos and diagrams that he will happily share with you.

I have the benefit of having learnt how to iron a parade uniform, while serving in the Army Reserve when I was much younger, however these days, all I iron are cotton shirts and the 'wash and wear' trousers I wear to the office.

If you're going to get into ironing, use a steam iron and an adjustable ironing board. Read the manual or visit Google to get an understanding of your iron.

When you're ready, the secret is to smooth out whatever it is you want to iron on the flat of the ironing board, and then go over it with a hot iron. Don't leave the iron in any one place for too long and you shouldn't have too many problems.

If you're ironing shirts, do the neck and shoulders first by drooping the shirt over the end of the ironing board.

Remember, the more often you do it, the better you'll become.

# OUTSOURCING

If it all seems too much, you can always consider outsourcing - paying someone else to do things for you.

I live in the suburban house, with its extensive garden, that served as our family home while our boys were growing up. Twenty years ago, when I was doing a masters degree and working full time, we got a gardener. I've still got a gardener (the same one actually), even though the degree only took me three years of part time study. It's not that I don't like gardening or don't know how to drive a lawnmower, because I do, but paying someone else to take care of the garden gives me time for doing other things, like writing or reading the paper.

In today's busy world, there are plenty of service providers out there making a living from helping the rest of us get by. Here are a few suggestions, if you're pressed for time or can't be bothered with the hands on approach I've outlined above:

- Caterers - if you want to entertain, or get your meals delivered if cooking is too much trouble.

- Cleaners - otherwise known as 'cleaning ladies' - take care of keeping the house clean and tidy for you.
- Gardeners - there's an army of guys only too willing to mow lawns and maintain garden beds for you.
- Laundry services - they'll do your washing and ironing, and give it back to you all neatly folded.
- Shopping - you place an order online or over the phone, someone else puts the stuff in a box, and they deliver. Some supermarkets do this, and there is an ever expanding range of online providers catering for people living in apartments in cities.

Google any of these services to get an idea of what's available for you in your neighbourhood. If you live in a small community, outsourcing may not be an option for some of these services.

The other side of outsourcing is cost. You need to weigh up the cost to benefit equation for each service, in light of the outcome of the discussion we'll have in the money management chapter.

Nothing comes for free.

# MONEY MANAGEMENT

*If you've always been the money manager in your household or you already have a money management plan, you can skip this section - unless you want a refresher on money management.*

**Know where the money goes**

I've read that women are either the money managers or the spending decision makers in the majority of households. If this was the case in your relationship, now that you're on your own, you need to take charge of your cash-flow.

There is one thing you need to understand about money. It's a form of energy that likes to keep moving. The secret is exercising some control over money's movements through your hands.

It won't take you long to work out how much money is flowing into your hands. Unless you're being paid in cash, all you need to do is take a look at your bank account statements and do the maths.

I suggest you work out how much money you receive each month, even if you get paid weekly or fortnightly.

The reason for doing it monthly is that the bills tend to arrive on regular monthly or quarterly cycles. For example, if you have a mobile (cell) phone on a plan the provider will send you a bill every month, and if you're connected to the internet, that provider also wants to be paid every month.

The next activity is the one most of us put off or don't do, which only leads to trouble. That activity is analysing your expenses so that you can see where all that money goes.

Start by examining your bank account or credit card statements to identify if you have any bills being 'direct debited' or paid automatically from that account or credit card, and write down the details.

Locate all the bills that were paid over the last year. If you don't have access to them, you need to start recording them for the next twelve months to see where the cash goes.

If you have no records here are a few things to consider:

**Regular - daily, weekly, monthly, quarterly or annually**

- Electricity
- Gas
- Water
- Rent/mortgage payments
- Health insurance
- Telephone
- Internet
- Cable TV
- Food
- Bus/train fares
- Rates/property taxes

**No set pattern**

- Car
- Cleaning supplies
- Clothes
- Entertainment
- Other

Now compare the flow of cash in with the flow of cash out each month. If you have access to a spreadsheet program, use that, otherwise use a piece of paper with the expenses listed down one side and the months across the top. If you're not good with numbers, locate a calculator - try the utilities folder on your smartphone - and add up the expenses for each month.

Don't be surprised if you discover that in some months the outflow exceeds the inflow.

This is where your budget or money management plan comes in. The idea behind budgeting is to get an understanding of your cash flows so that you can plan for known expenses in advance, and build up a buffer to cover the gap in those months when your outflow exceeds your inflow.

If you're using a credit card to cover those gaps, you need to start working on a savings plan to wean yourself off using the bank's money, which is another expense you'll have to pay at some point.

**Saving**

Many years ago I worked in banking and finance. My first foray into that field was in selling managed investment products, Then I worked as a lending officer for a bank.

Those experiences highlighted that most people live from pay day to pay day, and have very little set aside for contingencies or retirement. In Australia, where I live, the government forces people to save for their retirement through compulsory superannuation. Other countries have various social security schemes that workers pay into so they will receive a basic pension when they retire, provided their government doesn't follow the example of Greece.

The honest truth of the matter is, that when it comes to saving, you can be your own worst enemy. Making a savings plan and sticking to it requires self-discipline, and not only for making regular deposits into your savings account but also for resisting the temptation to buy stuff you can't afford and don't need.

To develop a savings plan you have to learn to live within your means. Living within your means is all about arranging your expenses so that they are less than your income. Not the same as - LESS THAN. Tell yourself you can do that, and then do it.

That's why you have to know where the money goes and when it goes there.

If you're spending money on drinks with the boys, gambling on the horses or with the pokies, burning it standing in the street (where else can you smoke these days?), buying takeaway food, keeping up with the latest fashion and going to the movies, and you're struggling to pay the rent each month, you have to take yourself to task and get your act together.

The challenge is to distinguish between essential and discretionary spending, and cut back the discretionary so that you can cover the essential. All those things in that list in the paragraph above - they fall under discretionary. Rent is an essential. Food is an essential.

The first part of your plan is to make sure you can cover the expenses that you can't avoid. That means being aware of what you're doing with your money every pay day.

One way to do it is to have two accounts: one for covering your living expenses and one for your savings. Set yourself a saving's target. Each time you get paid put 10 percent or more into the savings account. Give yourself an allowance to cover incidentals and make sure everything else goes into the living expenses account.

Pay your expenses out of the living expenses account. When you have money in your savings account or you have reached your saving's target, then you can indulge in those discretionary purchases that take your fancy.

Do yourself a favour and make a money management plan. You can't follow a plan that doesn't exist, and remember, it's a plan, so you can adjust it as your circumstances change.

# COOKING 4 ONE

# INTRODUCTION

This section contains a cookbook, written with the intention of helping you master the art of feeding yourself now that you're the one who has to do the cooking.

There are no intimidating pictures of perfectly prepared meals.

In fact, there is nothing fancy in this book at all.

This cookbook tells you how to cook the meals I discovered I could cook for myself, without having to decipher the secret language of all the fancy cookbooks on the shelf in the kitchen or available in bookstores or online.

When you look inside most cookbooks, the first thing you notice, after the glossy pictures, is that all the recipes (that's the fancy word for cooking instructions) are for preparing meals for two or more people. Not much help if you only want to cook for yourself, and you haven't done much of that before.

In this cookbook you'll find instructions for cooking 4 one.

For convenience, I've grouped the meals under the headings of breakfast, lunch and dinner, but you can eat any meal at any

## Introduction

sitting. It's your life. When you're living alone, if you want to eat a breakfast meal for dinner or vice versa, there's no-one there to complain or tell you to do otherwise.

Some meals could be listed under more than one heading. I've chosen the heading that makes sense to me.

Where possible, I focus on process so that you don't have to wade through a lot of repetition of the same instructions under different meal headings. For example, I look at pan frying (a process) instead of listing separate instructions for cooking steak, pork, sausages, chicken and fish.

If you've never cooked before, take comfort in the knowledge that if you can boil a pan of water on a cooktop, you already have one of the main skills required for success in the kitchen.

You also have a lot of other skills, like being able to read instructions and measure things, that will come in handy. If you're good at project management, some of those skills can be transferred to the kitchen as well.

The first part of the book covers buying and storing food, and a few other basic instructions I think you'll find helpful.

Towards the end of the book, I've included a chapter on entertaining, for those of you who want to cook a meal to share with friends - after you have the basics under the belt.

When you've mastered the basic cooking skills in this book, I encourage you to venture into some of those fancy cookbooks with the glossy pictures - they won't seem so intimidating once you have an idea of how this cooking thing works.

*Disclaimer:* I am not a chef or a nutritionist - although plenty of men are. I'm simply a practitioner. At the time of writing, I've been cooking for myself for around five years, using the ideas you'll find in this section.

# SOME BASIC STUFF

In this chapter we'll look at buying food and what to do with it once you get it home. We'll also take a brief look at the equipment you need for cooking and preparing meals.

## Buying food

You probably know where to go to buy food: the supermarket, the butcher's, the baker's, the greengrocer's or fruit and veg shop. If your life has been anything like mine, you've probably been sent down to one or more of those places with a list at some point in your life.

Now that you're on your own, the challenge is writing the list before you go. And, writing a list is essential, if you don't want to blow your budget or wind up with a lot of stuff that you'll end up throwing out.

I started by doing my food shopping in the supermarket, and moved out to the specialty stores, like the butcher and fruit and veg shop, once I had some degree of confidence that I knew what I was doing.

If you can't find something to eat in a supermarket, you're not looking. Not only do they stock the basic ingredients for the dishes you might want to cook, they also have prepared meals that only require the application of heat, and ready made salads that only need to be opened.

The first time you go to the supermarket, spend some time getting yourself oriented with the layout, so that you can structure your list to align with the layout as you move through the supermarket. This saves a bit of backtracking, but don't get too carried away because, every now and then, they shift things just to see if you're awake.

My preferred option is to cook but if you need to start with prepared meals, start there and progress to cooking.

**Shopping budget**

The other thing about shopping is to set a budget. How much do you want to, or how much can you afford to, spend on food? If you haven't been the one doing the shopping until now, you might get a surprise (shock) when you get to the checkout.

The thing to remember is that it's still cheaper to shop and cook than what it is to eat out, and it will probably be a lot better for your health as well.

**Basic shopping list**

In the parts of the book that cover specific meals, I provide you with a list of the ingredients required to make those meals. In this basic list, the focus is on the basic items you'll need to get through a week, so that you'll have some idea of how to put together a shopping list. I chose that time frame on purpose. I suggest you do your food shopping weekly, at least until you have worked out your own routine.

I'm an omnivore, so I'll cover the full range of foods. If you're a vegetarian or you have other dietary issues, feel free to adjust my suggestions or use Google - there are stacks of helpful sites out there; like 4 Ingredients, for example.

**Beverages:** tea, coffee, fruit juice and mineral water.

**Bread:** I generally have a loaf of sliced bread and a loaf of raisin bread on my list every second week. Sometimes, especially if I'm going to be home for lunch for a few days, I'll buy a packet of pita bread - the round flat stuff.

**Breakfast cereals:** instant rolled oats (oatmeal) and muesli (granola).

**Cheese:** grated parmesan to go with the pasta or rice dishes, and cheddar to go with the sliced ham.

**Condiments:** items like tomato sauce (ketchup), mustard and mayonnaise. And, don't forget butter or whatever spread you prefer, and salt - comes in handy when you're cooking pasta and rice.

**Cooking oils:** if you buy cooking oils, like olive oil, buy the small bottle - it starts going off once you open the bottle.

**Eggs:** buy a dozen every couple of weeks or get half a dozen each week. Eggs keep in the fridge.

**Fish:** if you're not into the red meat, pick up some fish. I usually buy frozen fish in the supermarket, a couple of slices of salmon always come in handy and it's easy to cook. Select individual serving sizes.

My other fish standby is tinned tuna - I keep four or five on the pantry shelf. They come in handy on those days when you forget to take something out of the freezer the night before.

**Fruit:** can go off, so don't buy too many of any particular type. I usually restrict myself to one container of strawberries, one peeled pineapple (why would you want to peel one yourself?) and five of any other fruit.

**Herbs and spices:** supermarkets have an extensive range of packaged herbs and spices. I buy the mixed Italian herbs, curry powder and cloves.

**Meat:** supermarkets have a display case of meats. Plan how many meat meals you will have in the coming week and choose from the display. Maybe some steak, some chicken and pork. It's all labelled, so it's what you see is what you get.

In addition to the meat I cook, I also buy sliced ham to use in my weekend lunches. That's usually found in the fridge next to the dairy products.

**Milk:** I buy the long life UHT milk that does not need to be stored in the fridge until after it is opened, and I buy the one litre or quart size. Milk's one of those things that can go off, so using smaller sized bottles or cartons is the way to go, unless you're a big milk drinker.

**Pasta:** this is one of my staples - when you marry an Italian you learn a lot about pasta. You can make a lot of different meals based on pasta. And, these days, there is an almost unbelievable range of pasta sauces available. All you have to do is either stir the sauce through your cooked pasta or simply heat up the sauce before adding to the cooked pasta. The other ingredient you'll need for pasta dishes is grated parmesan cheese.

**Rice:** if you can do it with pasta you can do it with rice, and there are a few things you can do with rice that you'd probably not do with pasta. In any case, both pasta and rice are easy to cook.

**Vegetables:** I'm a frozen vegetables guy. My experience is you'll end up throwing less stuff out if you buy frozen vegetables. I buy root vegetables like potatoes and carrots, green salads, tomatoes and capsicums in the fresh-food section but everything else comes out of the freezer. For the fresh stuff, I only buy what I know I'll eat that week. If I buy pumpkin, I buy a piece, preferably one that has already been peeled. In some shops, they even cut it up for you.

**Yogurt (Yoghurt):** this is my favourite for adding to fruit salad, porridge (oats) or muesli, and I always have two large containers of it in the fridge.

**Non food items:** paper towels, cling wrap, freezer paper, ziplock bags.

There's lots of other stuff in the supermarket that you can explore at your leisure, but you can keep yourself alive with the ingredients on this basic shopping list.

**Storing food**

Now that you've done the shopping, what do you do with all that stuff when you get it home?

**Bread** can be stored in the freezer. Before you freeze a loaf of sliced bread, either separate it into lots of two slices in ziplock bags or insert freezer paper between the slices and store it in the plastic bag it came in. Bread rolls can be frozen in ziplock bags. Frozen bread does not take long to thaw out and it can be placed straight into the toaster.

**Carrots and pumpkins** go in the fridge.

**Dairy products,** including butter, go into the fridge, but there are a couple of items that get special treatment. I store milk in the pantry because I buy the long-life UHT type. If you buy the other variety, put it in the fridge. Grated parmesan cheese - store enough for one or two servings in the fridge, put the rest in the freezer inside a plastic container with an airtight lid. If you keep it in the fridge for a long period it will go green - with mould.

**Frozen food** goes into the freezer as soon as you get it home. This obviously applies to frozen seafood and frozen vegetables. Nothing lasts forever, not even food that you store in a freezer. If you're not going to cook it within a couple of weeks, put a label on it and give it the sniff test when you thaw it out before cooking it. I have a pretty straight forward rule I follow: if in doubt, throw it out!

**Fruit juices and fruit** go in the fridge, however, if you buy bananas leave them in a bowl on the kitchen bench. If you bought strawberries, take them out of the container, transfer them into a paper towel lined plastic or glass container with a lid before putting them in the fridge. The paper towel absorbs moisture which might otherwise encourage mould.

**Meat** can be divided up into single servings - a piece of meat roughly the size of your hand, and slipped into ziplock plastic bags. If you're having a meat meal in the next 24 hours, put one bag in the fridge and the rest into the freezer. You can easily slip a label into a ziplock bag to keep track of the age of meat you put in the freezer. Of course, the real secret to avoiding food poisoning is to only buy what you're going to eat, so that you don't end up with old stuff in the freezer.

**Packaged items** like pasta, rice, breakfast cereals, condiments in unopened bottles and jars, tinned fish and the like can be stored in a cupboard or pantry. Another rule I adhere to is, never store stuff in the can once you have opened the can. Transfer what you didn't use into a glass or plastic container with a lid.

**Potatoes** can be stored in a basket or a bag in the pantry.

**Salads and tomatoes** go in the fridge, and if you bought the pre-washed green salad, the paper towel trick for strawberries works for the green salad as well. I usually leave the tomatoes in the plastic bag, but I do not tie off the bag.

### The 'if in doubt throw it out' rule

You do not want to give yourself food poisoning, so whenever you take something out of the fridge, thaw out food from the freezer, open a container or a packet, you need to be conscious of any funny smells. If it smells off, or has fluffy green or grey stuff growing on it, throw it out - no matter how much you paid for it!

### Equipment

Unless you're starting totally fresh in a new location, because she got the house and all the cooking utensils, you'll probably have access to all the cooking equipment you need. If not, go to a cookware or department store, after you've reviewed this section, and buy what you need. It's a lot of fun shopping in those stores, so make a list before you go. The good stuff is not cheap.

Here's what you're likely to find in the kitchen cupboards and drawers or need to buy.

**Knives** for cutting things up - at least one long bladed and one short bladed knife. Treat them with respect, as most kitchen knives designed for food preparation are sharp.

A **cutting board** or two for cutting things up on. Lots of people suggest you have separate boards for meat and other things.

**Utensils** like forks, serving spoons, egg turner/flipper, tongs, kitchen scissors and vegetable parer/peeler.

**Measuring** cups, spoons and jug. These are either plastic or metal, though the jug may be glass, and have numbers and words on them, for example ½ cup, teaspoon, ½ teaspoon, litres or pints.

A **kitchen scale**. If you have to buy one, get an electronic version. They're battery powered and a lot easier to read, especially if, like me, you need to put your glasses on to read any of this stuff.

A range of **saucepans** and **frying pans** (skillets) with lids. You might find a splatter guard you can use on a frying pan without a lid, and a **colander** to strain off water from food after cooking.

A range of **microwave dishes** of different shapes and sizes.

**Bowls** for mixing ingredients or holding salads.

You should also find a range of **appliances**, like a toaster, an electric kettle or jug, a sandwich maker and a lot of other stuff, like blenders and food processors, that you can read the instructions for later.

**Microwave oven** and **gas or electric cooktop**. Leave the **wall oven** for when you have discovered oven bags and want to explore roasts.

### Portion sizes

Portion size is all about exercising some control over the amount of food you consume. Paying attention to how much food you cook and put on your plate helps you keep the weight down. I find the easiest way to control how much I eat is to choose specific amounts or to use a specific measure of dry ingredients.

For example, for a meat meal I find one piece of meat or two sausages is usually enough, and for things like rice or porridge or muesli, I use half a cup.

Another method I use to control portion size is to cook all my vegetables in the one microwave dish.

**Variety**

Variety is meant to be the spice of life. Whether that's true or not could be the subject of another book, but it's certainly what makes eating interesting, and it supports what the nutritionists say.

This translates to developing a menu of dishes you can cook, so that you're not eating the same stuff all the time. I've provided some example menus for you to consider in the sample menus chapter.

# PREPARING MEALS

Some food is ready to eat when you get it home. You might have to wash it, cut it up and mix it with another food item, but you don't need to do anything special to it. I deal with this type of food under the heading: fresh food.

Other types of food need to go through a conversion process, associated with the application of heat, otherwise known as cooking.

**Fresh food**

Apart from the food items, all you need to prepare fresh food is a knife, a flat surface, like a cutting board, and a plate or bowl to serve the food in.

**Cold meats**

Those cold meats you picked up in the delicatessen section can be teamed with a salad or two, or added to a sandwich.

## Fruit

Many fruits only need a rinse under the tap and they're ready to eat. Some, like bananas, kiwis and oranges need peeling before you can eat them. The beauty with fruits is that you can cut them up and mix them together into a fruit salad. You might not want to eat a whole apple, a whole banana and a kiwi fruit all at once, so cut them in half and slip one half of each fruit into the fridge in a ziplock bag, and use that for tomorrow's fruit salad.

## Salads

These days you can buy a whole range of ready made salads, in addition to the traditional green salad, which now comes pre-washed and sealed in a bag or container. Some of these salads can be a meal in themselves. Others can be mixed with cold meats to make a meal in minutes.

## Sandwiches: bread, bread rolls, crackers and crispbreads

What you can do with a couple of pieces of bread is only limited by your imagination - everything from the humble peanut butter to a multi-layered cold meat, cheese and salad sandwich.

And, if you can do it with two pieces of sliced bread, you can do it with a bread roll or crackers and crispbreads.

## Yogurt (Yoghurt)

You can eat yogurt on its own or add it to your fruit salad for breakfast, lunch or dinner.

## Converting food into cooked meals

Cooking is not rocket science, but a little science and math will help.

To be successful as a cook, you need to be able to measure and weigh things, read dials or electronic displays, and control a heating flame or electric element.

If you're not into creative cooking, you need to be able to follow instructions in cook books, like this one.

## Cooking

If you have no idea, there are some fall back positions, like prepared meals that only need heating up or eating out, that you can use, but you'll be doing yourself a favour by learning to cook. It's not all that much of a mystery. If you're game, you can teach yourself the basics - if someone points you in the right direction, which is what I'm doing here.

Cooking is basically following instructions and paying attention. This means that if you can operate a TV or a computer or a smartphone, you can cook yourself a meal.

The thing with preparing a meal is it's a bit like project management. You have several things going on at once leading up to a final outcome. You want all the hot things ready at the same time, otherwise you end up with a less than satisfactory eating experience. The secret to a hot meal comes down to timing and doing things in the correct sequence. This calls for a little common sense planning.

For example, if you're preparing poached eggs on toast, you need to get the bread into the toaster just after you've put the eggs into the water in the pan, otherwise your eggs will be hard by the time you have your toast buttered, or your buttered toast will be rock hard by the time you have the eggs ready.

A lot of food, like frozen vegetables, pasta, rice, and baked beans, comes with instructions on the packet or container. Read them, pay particular attention to the suggested cooking time, and then do what they say. You'll get better with practice, and as you come to understand the behaviour of your microwave oven or cooktop.

You can make a lot of meals by cooking some pasta or rice and mixing it with a serving of cooked frozen vegetables or a can of tuna, or both, and don't forget all those pasta sauces you can buy.

If you're a meat eater, you can pan-fry steak, lamb, pork, chicken or fish and add a serving of salad or vegetables. Pan-frying most meats in a non-stick frying pan, with or without a lid, only takes five or six minutes. Allow three minutes on both sides, or leave it a bit longer if you prefer it well done. If you put it on the plate and discover it's underdone, put it back in the pan for a bit longer.

Experiment by putting a dash of olive oil or a dob of butter into the frying pan before you place the meat in the pan. Keep in mind that thicker slices of meat take longer to cook that thinner slices, and fish doesn't take as long as steak.

You've probably done some cooking on the BBQ, so you should have a basic idea about how to cook meat. If you haven't, the secret is low heat and patience, and when you cook meat inside, it pays to turn on the exhaust fan, if you have one, or to open a window if you don't. You can also minimise the spread of cooking smells by cooking your meat in a frying pan with a lid.

# BREAKFAST

Breakfast is an important meal, so try not to give into the temptation to skip it or grab something on the way to the office.

In my opinion, breakfast needs to be more than a cup of hot coffee, so in this chapter I'll cover several different ways of making something to eat for the first meal of the day.

**Toast**

Toast is one of the easiest things to make for breakfast. All you need to make toast is sliced bread and a toaster.

You can also make toast using crumpets, English muffins and raisin or fruit loaf. Some toasters have a special setting for toasting crumpets so you don't burn the bottom while toasting the top. You need to split English muffins in half before dropping them into a toaster.

Once you get your toast out of the toaster, you can add to its appeal by spreading butter and peanut butter or honey (or both), jam, nutella, or vegemite (if you're Australian). You're not restricted to these. Fresh avocado or chutney on toast can be a refreshing change.

My favourite toast breakfast is toasted raisin loaf spread with butter and honey.

Toast can be a meal on its own or a side dish in support of something else, like eggs or soup, or it can be used as the basis for a steak sandwich.

**Equipment notes**

As long as you have access to an electric toaster, you can make toast.

Remember, the toaster is connected to the mains electricity supply, so if your toast gets stuck in the toaster, turn it off at the wall before you start poking around inside the toaster with a knife. Electricity is one of those things it's better to have a healthy respect for - take it for granted and you might get more than a shock.

**Muesli**

Muesli, also known as granola in North America, is a mixture of oats and other cereals, dried fruit, and nuts. It comes in toasted and un-toasted or natural formats.

There is quite a range of mueslis, each with a different combination of cereals, dried fruits and nuts. There is even a variety without any dried fruit.

Muesli is even easier than toast, and takes less time to prepare. Simply tip ½ cup of muesli into a bowl and then add either milk or yogurt.

Enjoy. No cooking required.

## Equipment notes

Until you get your 'eye in', a half cup measure is the only specialized tool you need, and only if you want to control your portion size.

## Porridge

Porridge is made from rolled oats or oatmeal. I use the instant version - it takes less time to cook.

This is one of those meals where the ability to boil water in a pot on the stove comes in handy.

To make porridge, put a cup of water into a small non-stick saucepan, add ½ cup of rolled oats or oatmeal, stir with a wooden spoon or spatula, and bring to the boil on the cooktop. Turn down the heat when it starts to boil - to minimize the chance of a boil over.

Your porridge will be ready in a minute or so after it starts to boil. It's ready when it's 'creamy' and looks like porridge. This is a judgment call by you.

Scrape the porridge into a bowl and add milk or yogurt. If you have a sweet tooth, stir in a spoonful of honey or sprinkle sugar on top.

Some people cook their porridge in milk instead of water. Give it a try, you might like it that way.

I find plain porridge a bit boring, so I toss a sliced up banana or a handful of dried apricots into the porridge as it's cooking. I usually add three or four spoonfuls of yogurt to the mixture once it's in the bowl.

## Equipment notes

Use a small non-stick saucepan. By small, I mean one that will hold around a litre or a quart of liquid.

Wooden spoons or plastic spatulas do not scratch the inside of non-stick saucepans.

## Other Breakfast Cereals

Muesli and porridge are my favourites, but there are other wheat or corn based breakfast cereals out there. They're all easy to prepare. Just add milk. Most of them already have more than enough sugar in them, and you can always add fruit like banana or strawberries.

## Eggs

There are two ways you can cook eggs just by adding them to water and applying heat.

### Hard or soft-boiled eggs.

The difference between soft and hard-boiled eggs is the time the eggs spend in hot water.

Put enough water into a small saucepan so that when you gently place two eggs into the water, the eggs are completely covered with water. Then put the saucepan on the stovetop and either light the flame or turn on the heat. If you like your eggs really runny, take them out as soon as the water boils. If you prefer them soft-boiled, leave them in the boiling water for one or two minutes, then take them out. If you like them hard-boiled, leave them in the boiling water for three minutes or more. This is one place you can experiment until you work it out without ruining your food. If you leave it too long, the eggs will still be edible.

I use a tablespoon to lift the eggs out of the water and place them into a small bowl, before transferring them one at a time into the eggcup. Be careful. Freshly boiled eggs are hot. Use a knife to slice off the top, add your condiment of choice, and use a teaspoon to scoop out the egg.

**Note:** cold hard-boiled eggs can also be a useful addition to a salad. It's best to cool them down under running water before attempting to peel them. You can peel a hard-boiled egg by cracking the shell all over and rolling it between your hands.

**Poached eggs**

Half to three quarter fill a frying pan with cold water, add a couple of drops of vinegar (stops the white spreading) and place it on the stove top. Turn on the heat.

Crack two eggs on the side of the frying pan, one at a time, and put them into the water. If you have trouble cracking eggs on the side of the frying pan, like I do, crack them on the side of a small bowl or cup and then tip them into the water.

Again, the longer you leave the eggs in the water, the harder they will become. When the eggs are cooked to your preferred consistency, use an egg turner/flipper to lift them out of the pan and transfer them to your plate.

I like to eat my soft poached eggs on toast, so as soon as I have the eggs in the water, I put two slices of bread in the toaster. By the time the eggs are ready, I have two pieces of buttered toast waiting for them on the plate.

To stop dripping water over your toast, tip the water out of the pan before you lift out the eggs.

**Fried eggs**

If you use a non-stick frying pan, fried eggs are poached eggs cooked without using water. If you're not using a non-stick frying pan, heat up some butter in the pan before you drop in the eggs.

**Scrambled eggs**

Scrambled eggs are a little more complicated, but not much. Crack two eggs into a small bowl, add a dob of butter, two tablespoons of milk - more if you prefer, pepper and salt to taste, and then whisk the contents of the bowl with a fork. Whisk is a fancy term for mixing together by stirring quickly. If you want to get fancy, there are special utensils called whisks you can use, but a fork will do the job.

Place a non-stick frying pan on the stovetop, turn on the heat and pour in the contents of the bowl. Turn down the heat, and stir with a plastic spatula or wooden spoon, until there is no liquid left. Takes about two minutes. Serve on toast.

**Things you can add to eggs for a more complete meal**

Eggs can be a meal on their own but you can easily add a few items to embellish your meal.

I've already mentioned toast, but you can poach or fry tomatoes with your eggs in the same frying pan. Simply cut up the tomato and drop it in with the eggs.

If you're doing fried eggs, you can also fry some bacon in the same pan. If you want to eat sausages with your eggs, cook the sausages first and then put the eggs into the pan when the sausages are nearly done.

Baked beans are a good companion for either poached of fried eggs. Simply empty a small can of baked beans into a non-stick saucepan and heat them up while you're preparing the eggs and toast.

## Equipment notes

Use a non-stick frying pan for cooking eggs, and if you scramble, poach or fry eggs use the egg flipper to give the bottom of the frying pan a quick clean as soon as you have lifted out the eggs.

## Fruit salad

Fruit is easy to turn into breakfast.

You can simply eat a banana or an orange or an apple or a peach for breakfast. Or you can make a fruit salad for breakfast by cutting up various fruits and mixing them together.

In places, like New York City and Adelaide, where I have shopped, you can buy prepared fresh fruit salad in the supermarket or greengrocers - no peeling or cutting required.

If you want to make a fruit salad using a variety of fruits, say strawberries, kiwi fruit, apple and banana but don't want to use a whole banana or apple or orange, simply cut the apple or banana or orange in half and slip the unused half into a ziplock bag. Store it in the refrigerator for later - just slice off the brown bit at the end of the banana before you cut it up for your next fruit salad.

You can eat fruit salad on its own, you can squeeze an orange over the mix, or cover it with yogurt or cream.

By purchasing a range of different fruits you can create an almost endless variety of fruit salad mixes.

Remember to try all the berries, grapes, pineapple and other fruits as they become available. You don't have to stick to the same ones each week.

## Equipment notes

A cutting board and a knife are all you need, and some ziplock bags if you want to store pieces of cut fruit for later.

## Beverages

### Fruit juices

Buy fruit juices at the supermarket. Store them in the fridge and start the day with a glass of your favourite juice. If you prefer squeezing fresh oranges in the morning, buy yourself a bag of oranges when you go shopping.

I do the squeezing fresh oranges thing during the winter months, when the tree in my yard is loaded, otherwise I buy fruit juice every week at the supermarket.

### Tea and Coffee

With the invention of the tea bag, all that's required for a cup of tea is boiling water and a little patience. I hear some people like to add milk and sugar to their tea.

Making coffee is also pretty easy and you have several options.

Instant coffee - drop a spoonful into a cup or mug and add boiling water, with milk and sugar to taste.

You can also add instant coffee to hot milk to make a latte style coffee for breakfast. I do this one with the microwave. I heat the milk in the microwave oven first, for seventy seconds (or on the beverage setting when I'm in New York), and then stir in the coffee. If you want to try this method, I suggest you experiment with your microwave oven to get the timing right - be prepared for a few messes until you work it out.

You can also heat the milk using a milk saucepan on the stove.

French press or coffee plunger - drop a scoop of ground coffee into the container and add boiling water. Insert the press/plunger and let it brew for a minute or three. Then slowly push the press/plunger to the bottom of the container and pour the contents into your cup. Unless you drink lots of coffee, a small french press designed for one makes ample coffee to start the day.

One other coffee making item I use is an Italian style coffee percolator, which brews ground coffee by forcing boiling water through the coffee under pressure. You can get these in one or two cup sizes – and much larger ones for entertaining.

Check when you're buying ground coffee that it's suitable for the method you want to use - french press/coffee plunger or percolator. If you're really keen, you can buy coffee beans and grind your own.

**Equipment notes**

Using an electric kettle or jug for boiling water is less of a risk than boiling water in a saucepan and then tipping it into a cup.

You can get carried away with coffee making with all the flash, easy to use coffee making machines on the market these days. If you want to go down that pathway, I'll leave it to you to read the instructions that come with the machine.

**Yogurt (Yoghurt)**

Yogurt can be added to cereals, porridge or fruit salads or eaten on its own.

I have to confess that yogurt is one of my favourite foods. It comes plain, flavoured and mixed with fruit pieces.

Greek style yogurt can also be used as a salad dressing. Try mixing it with cut up cucumber as a side salad with cooked meat dishes, or adding it to cooked mixed vegetables or baked and mashed potatoes.

One of the fun things about cooking is that you are allowed to experiment.

# LUNCH

In some parts of the world the midday meal or lunch is the main meal of the day.

I come from a part of the world where lunch is generally a light meal and dinner, eaten in the evening, is the main meal. If you're looking for something more substantial for lunch, feel free to use the ideas I have included in the dinner chapter.

**Sandwiches**

Sandwiches come in two main varieties: open and closed.

An open sandwich has one supporting layer, while a closed sandwich has a top and bottom layer.

The supporting layer can be composed of sliced bread, bread rolls, pita bread, crispbreads or crackers.

Pita bread (round, flat bread), crispbreads and crackers are ideal supports for open sandwiches. All you do is pile your chosen ingredients on top.

Sliced bread and bread rolls are the traditional supports for closed sandwiches. You end up with your ingredients in between layers of bread. If you use a bread roll, you can cut it horizontally into two halves or slice it so that it hinges open to take your filling.

Of course, you can convert an open sandwich made with pita bread into a closed sandwich by folding the bread, once you have the ingredients in place.

If you freeze your bread, remember to take out what you need the night before and let it thaw out overnight in the fridge. You can thaw a piece of frozen pita in the microwave oven - takes somewhere between ten and twenty seconds - but be warned, if you overdo it you get a very dry piece of bread. If you forget to take out the sliced bread, toast it.

**Ingredients or sandwich fillings**

What can you put into a sandwich? How long is a piece of string?

You can make a sandwich with any fresh, conserved, preserved or cooked food item you have available. It all depends on what you're prepared to eat with bread.

The filling for my standard weekend lunch sandwich is: a layer of butter, followed by a layer of chutney, a slice of ham, a slice of cheese, a couple of pieces of lettuce and a slice of tomato piled onto a piece of pita bread. Sometimes I use an Italian bread roll.

If I feel like indulging myself, I buy prosciutto, sun-dried tomatoes or spiced olives in oil and an Italian cheese, which is easy to do in my neighbourhood where we have shops catering to the tastes of the families of Italian immigrants.

You can make a simple sandwich with fresh bread and peanut butter.

Another easy to make open sandwich is a tuna sandwich. Simply empty a tin of tuna onto a piece of buttered bread. If you don't want it to be soggy, drain the liquid from the can before adding the tuna to the bread.

Another variation I use is to toast the bread before I make the sandwich. If you have time, cook up a piece of steak and make yourself a steak sandwich, by putting the cooked meat between two pieces of toast with some salad. If you're really hungry you can also fry an egg to add to that steak sandwich.

Be creative and experiment. If it's edible on its own you can add it to bread to make a sandwich, and you won't know what any combination tastes like unless you try it.

**Equipment notes**

Once you have decided on your ingredients, generally all you need is a knife and a plate or a cutting board.

If you have access to a sandwich toaster, you can toast the bread with the ingredients already inside. Read the instructions, or experiment with timing, to avoid overcooking your sandwich.

**Fresh Salads**

There are no set rules for making a fresh salad. Basically all you do is cut up and mix together your chosen ingredients.

The easiest salad to make is a mixed green salad. This is a combination of different lettuce leaves and baby spinach leaves, which you can buy as a pre-washed mixture in a sealed bag or container. All you have to do is take some out of the bag, put it on the plate and add your salad dressing of choice.

You can create a slightly more sophisticated version by adding some cut up tomato and cucumber to the green leaves, or maybe some thinly sliced carrot or cut up celery.

This is one food item you can be creative with.

If you want to sweeten a salad add a few slices of apple and/or pear. If you want a bit more body, cut up some cheese and throw it into the mix, or open a can of tuna and mix that in. If you buy the Italian style tuna it comes with its own olive oil based salad dressing.

There are lots of different types of cheese you can try in a salad, and don't forget those slices of cold meat you picked up from the delicatessen section in the supermarket. You can also add things like sliced olives or sun-dried tomatoes, which come in their own olive oil based salad dressing.

**Salad dressing for fresh food salads.**

You can use Greek yogurt, mayonnaise, or any of the prepared salad dressings available in the supermarket. It's not that difficult to make your own salad dressing using olive oil or balsamic vinegar, or a mixture of both, with some black pepper and salt - just tip it onto the salad straight out of the bottle and then add the pepper and salt.

Or make your own vinaigrette - that's one of those fancy words you find in cookbooks for salad dressing. An easy vinaigrette can be made using freshly squeezed lemon juice, Dijon mustard, olive oil and salt.

Use twice as much olive oil as lemon juice, a teaspoon or less of the mustard and salt to taste. Add the olive oil to the lemon juice in a cup or other small container, stir in the mustard and add salt to taste. Spoon the result over your salad.

If you make too much, put the excess in a sealed container in the fridge and use it next time. And if you can't find a fresh lemon, they sell lemon juice in bottles these days - remember to keep the bottle in the fridge once you open it.

**A word of warning.**

If you make too much salad, put the excess into a container to store in the fridge before you put the salad dressing onto the salad. Dressed salads made from fresh ingredients become a soggy mess overnight.

**Equipment notes**

A cutting board and a knife, and a small container and a spoon to make your vinaigrette.


**Cold meats**

Those cold meats you picked up in the delicatessen section in the supermarket can be teamed with a salad or two to make a meal, or used as a sandwich filler.

If you freeze your sliced ham or beef or chicken or turkey, remember to take some out of the freezer and let it thaw out in the fridge overnight.

And, try some of the continental meats like prosciutto or salami. There is quite a range of cold meats available, so be brave and experiment.

# DINNER

This chapter covers processes for making more substantial meals. I've also included a few easy to follow recipes - instructions for making specific meals.

### Making Soup

I'm not a big soup maker but I have learnt to cook a couple of soups.

### Frozen vegetable soup

I discovered this soup when I started cooking for myself. Not being a big fan of peeling and cutting up vegetables, I decided to see what I could do with a packet of frozen vegetables - someone else has already peeled and cut them up for you. I ended up with several versions.

The basic ingredients for making this soup are:

- 1 kilogram (around 2 pounds) frozen mixed vegetables - this is one of the standard size packets in Australia. You

get different soups simply by using different combinations of frozen vegetables.
- 3 or 4 stock cubes - chicken, beef or vegetable. You get different tastes depending on which type of stock cube you use.

Method:

Empty the packet of frozen vegetables into a deep saucepan. No need to thaw them out. Add two litres (2 quarts) of water and then throw in the stock cubes of your choice. Give the mix a stir and put the lid on the saucepan.

If you want a slightly different texture, add 500 grams (a pound) of cut up beef or chicken to the mix before you start cooking the soup.

Place the saucepan on the cooktop and bring to the boil, then turn down the heat and let it simmer for around an hour.

When it's cooked, let it cool, give it a stir and then divide the soup into several plastic containers with lids that you can store in the freezer. You will have enough soup for three meals.

Serving:

This is a fairly basic soup, so I usually serve it with pasta or rice. Cook up a cup or two of pasta or half a cup of rice, while you are gently reheating the soup. Strain the pasta or rice and add to the soup. Sprinkle some grated parmesan cheese on top before enjoying.

If you want something a little more exotic, try using beef or chicken ravioli instead of plain pasta.

## Pumpkin soup

This is a winter favourite I learnt to cook many years ago, so I have a formal recipe for this one.

Ingredients:

- 2 onions
- 1 sweet potato
- 4 carrots
- 1 medium sized butternut pumpkin (or 2 pumpkin halves)
- 4 chicken stock cubes
- 1 teaspoon of curry powder - more if you like it hot!
- 1 tin of coconut cream
- Generous dash of sweet chilli sauce - can be added when served instead of going into the pot.

Method:

Peel the onions, sweet potato, carrots and pumpkin and cut them into chunks.

Place the chopped up vegetables into a deep saucepan, add the chicken stock cubes, the curry powder and the coconut cream. You can add the sweet chilli sauce at this point or leave it to when you serve. Add sufficient water to cover the vegetables, stir with a wooden spoon and then put the lid on the saucepan.

Place the saucepan on the cooktop and bring to the boil, then turn down the heat and let it simmer until the vegetables are tender. Takes at least an hour.

When cooked, puree using a blender. I let it cool before doing this part. Divide the resultant soup into several plastic containers with lids that you can store in the freezer. You will have enough soup for several meals.

Serving:

Tip the soup into a small saucepan and heat gently until it starts to boil, then transfer it to your soup bowl. If you didn't add the sweet chilli sauce when you made the soup, add a dash now and stir it in. You can also chop up some parsley to sprinkle on top, or stir in a spoonful of yogurt or sour cream. Salt to taste.

**Equipment notes**

Use a deep saucepan with a lid for making soup. If you're using a gas cooktop, you might need to use a flame or heat diffuser to reduce the heat to a low enough simmer. Set some sort of reminder or stay in the kitchen, because it's fairly easy to boil a pot dry if you go off and do something else and forget about it.

**Pasta and Rice dishes**

When I was a kid, spaghetti came in a can. Then I married an Italian - and discovered a whole new world of pasta.

If you can boil water in a saucepan you can cook pasta. If you can cook pasta you will never go hungry, and you'll be able to impress your mates (buddies) with your culinary skills.

When I was introduced to cooking pasta my wife's family was still making their own pasta sauce. These days, there are so many varieties of pasta sauce available in the supermarket or speciality Italian food stores, you can enjoy the wide world of pasta without having to know anything about making specialty sauces. You don't even have to like tomatoes. There are plenty of other sauces to choose from. My only advice is buy the small jar - it usually holds enough sauce for two or three serves - unless you're entertaining.

## Pasta with sauce

Use a saucepan large enough to hold 2 litres (2 quarts) of water and two-thirds fill it with water. If you're cooking spaghetti, use a deeper saucepan or break the spaghetti into shorter lengths.

Add a teaspoon of salt to the water, put the lid on the saucepan and bring it to the boil. When the water's boiling, remove the lid and add 1½ - 2 cups of dry pasta to the boiling water. If you're cooking spaghetti, use between a quarter to a third of the contents of the packet. The cooking time recommended on the packet starts once the water starts to boil again. Be prepared to turn down the heat and to give the pasta an occasional stir.

How do you tell when pasta is cooked? The best way is to taste it. When it tastes right to you, that's when it's cooked. You've possibly heard of 'pasta al dente' - that's pasta that meets the bite test as far as you are concerned, as you're the one who will be eating it. Like everything else in life, a little practice goes a long way, and if you overcook pasta it's simply a little softer than expected.

When it's cooked, drain the water from the pasta by tipping the contents of the saucepan into a colander. Shake out the excess water and return the pasta to the saucepan. Stir in a couple of tablespoons or your chosen sauce and serve with grated parmesan cheese.

## Pasta with anything else

Another thing about pasta is that you aren't restricted to eating it as a meal on its own with pasta sauce.

You can add it to cooked vegetables or soups. You can tip stewed meat and vegetables onto it. You can add it to a curry. You can mix it with a can of tuna in olive oil or, like Inspector West, in my novel *The Holiday,* you can make pasta marinara by adding mixed seafood, lightly cooked in olive oil and garlic. You'll find the seafood mix either at the fish market or in the freezer at the supermarket.

You cook the pasta as described above and then mix it with whatever else you have cooked.

If you want to try pasta marinara, put the pasta in the pot first and while it's cooking, prepare the seafood mix in a frying pan. Start by heating a small amount of crushed garlic in a dash of olive oil. When the garlic sizzles, tip in a cup or two of the seafood mix and stir with a wooden spoon. It only takes a few minutes to cook. If you like, you can add a few slices of fresh tomato to the garlic and oil before you add the seafood.

I never put cheese on pasta with seafood, whether that seafood is the marinara mix or tuna in olive oil from a can.

**Rice**

Anything you can do with pasta you can do with rice.

The differences between cooking rice and pasta are you need less rice, usually ½ cup of dry rice is plenty for one person, you only need about a litre (quart) of water in the saucepan, and you don't need to wait for the water to boil before you tip the rice into the saucepan. I add a teaspoon of salt to the water before tipping in the rice.

You do, however, need to be a little more vigilant to make sure the saucepan doesn't boil over. Again, you need to apply a taste test to determine when it's cooked. When it's cooked, strain it with a colander just like you do for the pasta.

You can enjoy rice with all those pasta sauces, and all those other things I suggested you mix with pasta.

## Equipment notes

Medium sized saucepan with a capacity of at least 2 litres or quarts, a colander and a measuring cup.

I short circuit the measuring cup part by using a small bowl that I know holds sufficient dry pasta to satisfy my appetite when cooked. I always use the measuring cup with rice.

Pays to rinse out the colander with hot water immediately after use.

## Pan-frying

We should be forever grateful to those people who pioneered the application of teflon to cooking utensils. They invented a man's best friend in the kitchen - the non-stick frying pan.

All you need to cook in a non-stick frying pan is a stove or cook-top. In other words, the application of heat. You don't even need a lid for the frying pan but using one helps keep the frying fat within the pan.

Pan-frying is a bit like having a small indoor barbecue.

### Whole pieces of meat or fish

To pan-fry a fillet (a fleshy boneless piece) of steak, pork, lamb, chicken or fish or a steak, pork or lamb chop ( a thick slice of meat with a piece of bone in it) all you do is place the frying pan on the cooktop, ignite or turn on the heat - low to moderate setting - and drop the piece of meat into the frying pan. After around three minutes, less if it's a thin fillet, more if its a really thick chop, flip it over using a fork or tongs and cook the other side.

You know how you like your meat cooked. If you want it rare, reduce the cooking time. If you want it well done, increase the cooking time. Turning up the heat does not speed up cooking - it burns the outside. Low heat is best for cooking meat and fish. Might take a little longer but you won't be eating charcoal.

**Pieces of meat**

Another way of cooking things like chicken breast or thighs or pieces of steak is to cut the meat into slices before you put it into the frying pan. You need to stir it with a wooden spoon or turn it over with tongs while it's cooking.

**Cooking meat in olive oil or butter**

If you want to vary the taste, try cooking your meat in either a dash of olive oil or a dob of butter, with or without sprinkling some dried herbs on top. Put the olive oil or butter into the heated pan before you place the meat into the pan. Sprinkle any dried herbs on while the meat's cooking. That's how it was done before we invented the non-stick frying pan.

**Marinating your meat - soaking it in a tenderizing liquid**

Another easy way of enhancing the taste of red meat, chicken or fish is to marinate it in a mixture of vinegar, lemon juice or wine, olive oil and fresh or dried herbs. You need to prepare the marinade (that's the fancy word for the mixture) and pour it over the meat several hours before you want to cook it for the best results.

Here are a couple of quick marinades for one that you can try. (There are plenty more online. Just ask Google.)

Marinade one.

In a glass or small bowl mix: ¼ cup olive oil, ½ cup of cider vinegar (or juice of a lemon), a pinch of salt, sprinkling of ground pepper and dried herbs.

Marinade two.

In a glass or small bowl mix: ½ cup soy sauce and a teaspoon of honey.

Place your meat in a dish or bowl and pour the marinade over the meat. Cover with cling wrap and place in the fridge for at least an hour, preferably longer. Overnight is good.

When you're ready to cook, pour the whole lot into your pan and cook on low heat.

## Sausages

You can pan-fry sausages, but I highly recommend using a lid on the frying pan. Sausages cook better if you do not prick them with a fork before cooking. These days the casings are designed to cook the sausage in its own fat content within the casing. But they can still make a mess. Again, medium to low heat works best.

For a slightly different taste, try cooking sausages in water in a saucepan or deep frying pan.

## Equipment notes

Use a small non-stick frying pan with a lid. If you don't use the lid, remember to turn on the exhaust or extractor fan or open a window. Cleaning the pan as soon as you have finished cooking, especially if you have used a marinade, is a good idea. At least fill it with water and let it soak while you eat if you don't.

## Cooked Salads

### Potato salads

One of my favourite cooked salads is potato salad. You can serve it hot or cold.

Peel two potatoes and dice them - cut them up into small cubes. Put them in a microwave dish with some water and cook them in the microwave for around four to five minutes. When they're cooked, drain the water and tip the cooked potato into a bowl. Mix in a tablespoon of mayonnaise. Eat or allow to cool - you can put the salad in the fridge to cool but remember to cover it with some cling warp. If you want a slightly different taste, use Greek yogurt instead of mayonnaise, or try stirring in a dob of butter and sprinkling on some mixed Italian herbs.

If you want a more sophisticated potato salad, cook up some frozen peas or corn or mixed vegetables and mix them in with the potatoes before you add the mayonnaise or yogurt or butter and spices.

If you cook potatoes using the more traditional pot of boiling water on the stove method, don't dice the potatoes until after you've cooked them, otherwise they will disintegrate in the pot. It takes around twenty minutes to cook whole or halved peeled potatoes in a pot of boiling water on the stove. You need to turn down the heat once the water is boiling and keep an eye on them - otherwise you'll end up with a mess.

Another ingredient you can add to a potato salad is hard-boiled eggs.

In fact, you can make a whole meal out of a potato salad by adding a can of tuna or by cutting up two cooked sausages and mixing them in to become part of the salad.

**Frozen vegetable salads**

This is another type of salad you can enjoy either hot or cold and it only takes a few minutes to prepare.

Put sufficient frozen vegetables into a microwave dish with some water, cover and microwave for between three and five minutes, depending on the strength of your microwave oven. When the vegetables are cooked, drain the water - tip them into a strainer if your microwave dish doesn't have a basket you can lift out - and watch out, the water will be hot! Then place the vegetables either on the plate or into a bowl and mix in the mayonnaise or yogurt or butter and spices.

You can do this using one type of vegetable, for example peas, or using a mixed vegetables selection. Where I shop, you can get various versions of the mixed vegetables. Try them all.

By the way, if you prefer a fresh salad with your main meal, refer to the fresh salads in the lunch chapter.

**Roasts**

I have access to an electric wall oven. I don't use it much. About the only thing I cook in it is roast chicken or leg of lamb with vegetables, and generally only if I'm entertaining as you get two or three meals worth of meat from a small chicken or leg of lamb. If you want to do roast chicken for one, use chicken parts instead of a whole chicken.

The secret to cooking a roast is the oven bag. The only special ingredient you need for cooking in an oven bag is plain flour. The oven bags come in a box with instructions printed on it.

The instructions cover things like oven temperature and cooking time by weight of the meat you want to cook and the type of oven - gas or electric.

Method:

- weigh the chicken or leg of lamb
- work out the required oven temperature and cooking time

- turn on the oven and preheat it to the required temperature
- rub some olive oil over the meat and sprinkle on some dried herbs - this bit is optional but enhances the taste
- add a tablespoon of plain white flour to the oven bag and give it a shake to spread it around
- place the meat into the bag
- wash and cut in half a potato, a carrot and an onion
- place the cut up vegetables into the bag around the meat - you can add a sprig of a fresh herb, for example, a bit of rosemary or basil instead of using the dried herbs mentioned above
- tie off the open end of the bag with the tie supplied - you might have to separate it from the bag
- place the bag into a baking dish or tray, and
- make a few holes in the top of the bag with a skewer or sharp pointed knife or a BBQ fork - stops it exploding.

When the oven is at the required temperature, place the dish or tray holding the bag onto the middle shelf of the oven, close the oven door and leave it for the required cooking time.

When it's cooked (the brown color gives it away), take the dish or tray out of the oven and put it onto a heat resistant surface - wooden cutting boards are good for this purpose. Slit the bag with a knife or cut it open with the kitchen scissors and transfer the contents to a large plate. You have the complete meal in the bag, unless you want to add a bit of salad.

Serve and enjoy.

If you have cooked more than you can eat, put the excess on a plate and cover with cling wrap and store in the fridge. You've got tomorrow's lunch or main meal ready.

## Equipment notes

Another benefit of using an oven bag, apart from the taste of eating meat cooked in its own juices, it's easy to clean up the baking dish or tray. All it needs is a rinse.

## Stews and Curries

In my kitchen, a stew is a mixture of stewing beef or steak and vegetables cooked together in the same pot with a liquid binder.

### Peter's beef stew

Ingredients:

- 250 - 300 grams (around half a pound) of boneless stewing beef or steak cut into cubes. You can buy it that way at the supermarket or ask the butcher to cut it up for you. Alternatively, use ground or minced beef - or try lamb or chicken instead of beef.
- Tablespoon of olive oil
- ¼ teaspoon of crushed garlic
- 1 large onion
- 1 large potato
- 2 cups of mixed frozen vegetables - peas, corn, carrots
- 1 cup of beef stock
- Salt, ground black pepper and dried herbs or fresh herbs like basil.

Method:

Peel the onion and slice it up. Place the sliced up onion in a small bowl. Note: either put the onion in the fridge for 15 minutes before you peel it, or peel under cold water in the sink or a bowl.

Peel the potato and cut it into chunks and put that in a separate bowl.

Make the beef stock using a ¼ beef stock cube and hot water in a coffee mug.

Put the pot onto the cooktop, turn on the heat - moderate heat works best. Tip the olive oil into the saucepan.

Place the meat into the saucepan, sprinkle in a pinch of salt, some ground black pepper and the dried herbs, and stir with a wooden spoon until the meat browns on all sides - around five minutes

Add the garlic and the onion and continue stirring until the onion softens - around three minutes.

Add the beef stock and potato and bring the mixture to the boil. Reduce the heat to low, tip in the mixed vegetables, give it a stir and cover. Let it simmer for at least half and hour.

If you think your stew is too runny, stir in a teaspoon of plain flour to thicken it up. If it dries out because you had the heat too high, add some more beef stock or water.

While the stew is cooking, cook up ½ cup of rice to serve with the stew. If you don't feel like rice, another easy serving option is toast.

## Curries

A curry is a stew with a twist. Instead of using beef stock, you use a small tin of coconut cream. Instead of dried herbs and garlic, you add a teaspoon of curry powder when the meat is browned. Another point of difference with a curry is you can add some fruit. Try adding sliced apple in with the onion or throw in some sultanas or dried apricots with the mixed vegetables.

If you want to try Thai green curry paste instead of the traditional curry, use chicken instead of beef.

**Equipment notes**

Use a mid-sized saucepan or stewing pot with a lid, and a wooden spoon for stirring. The recipe makes a stew for one, so if you use too large a pot the stock will be spread too thinly.

**Fish in the microwave**

Most times I cook fish I use the pan-frying option, especially if I have a thick tuna steak.

However, when I have a small piece of salmon, I usually cook it in the microwave.

You need a special microwave dish to cook fish in a microwave - a long, flat, three piece one: a tray with a separate perforated shelf (to keep the fish above the water in the bottom of the tray) and a lid.

It takes three minutes to cook a small piece of salmon in my microwave.

Squeeze some lemon juice onto the fish and enjoy with a salad or vegetables.

**Equipment notes**

Use an egg flipper to lift the cooked fish off the perforated shelf, otherwise it may break into bits if you try to lift it with a fork.

## Vegetables

### Cooking frozen vegetables

The quickest and easiest way to cook frozen vegetables is in the microwave.

Open the packet, tip a cup or two of frozen vegetables into a microwave dish with some water, cover and cook in the microwave for between four and six minutes. Read the cooking instructions on the packet and experiment with your microwave until you find the time that works best for you.

If you don't have a microwave, you can cook frozen vegetables in boiling water. Boil a small saucepan of water and tip the desired amount of frozen vegetables into the boiling water. Turn down the heat once the water starts boiling again and cook for two or three minutes. Adding a small amount of salt to the water enhances the taste for those of us that like a bit of salt. Again, read the instruction on the packet.

Using either method, drain the water from the cooked vegetables and serve. I usually stir in a dob of butter with pepper and salt, but you can add mayonnaise or Dijon mustard or Greek yogurt or olive oil as well.

### Cooking fresh vegetables

The quickest and easiest way to cook fresh vegetables is in the microwave.

Fresh vegetables take a little longer if you cook them whole or in large pieces. A whole potato, for example can take up to ten minutes depending on the power of the microwave and the size of the potato. Before you commit a whole potato to the microwave score it with a knife to break its surface. Fresh vegetables must be placed in a microwave dish with some water and covered.

You can cook a potato in the same dish as frozen mixed vegetables - provided you slice it up first.

If you don't have a microwave, you can cook fresh vegetables in boiling water. Place the vegetable whole or in bits into a saucepan with sufficient water to cover the vegetables, add salt if desired and apply heat. Once the water boils, turn down the heat. It takes around twenty minutes to cook most vegetables.

Again, when cooked, drain the water and serve with your choice of condiment.

To peel or not to peel? Your call. You can eat potatoes and carrots without peeling them. If you want to prepare mashed potatoes (or smashed potatoes as my sons called them when they were little), I suggest you peel the potatoes before you cook them.

By the way, you don't need any fancy equipment to mash potatoes. A fork will do the trick. Add a dash of milk, a dob of butter, salt and pepper to cooked potato pieces in a small saucepan or bowl and mash with a fork. If you want it fluffy, whip that fork around quicker or work out how to use the Mixmaster, if you have one. Too much washing up if you ask me.

You can also roast vegetables like potatoes, carrots and pumpkin. I usually only do that as part of a roast meal, as discussed above in the section on roasts.

**Equipment notes**

Microwave cooking generates very hot water, including steam, so exercise care when opening microwave dishes you have taken from the oven. You can buy microwave dishes that have a basket or separate part to hold the vegetables that makes it easier to get the cooked product out.

The best time to wash a microwave dish is just after you have emptied its contents onto your plate. Usually only requires a quick rinse under running water.

If you are using the more traditional method of boiling in a saucepan of water on the cooktop, stay vigilant. If you get distracted, burnt vegetables created by the pot boiling dry not only smell, they also create a cleaning headache you can do without.

**Stewed Fruit**

One of the few things I can remember my father cooking is stewed apricots. We'll cover the other cooking skill he taught me in the next section.

Fruit is easy to turn into an enjoyable dessert dish by stewing. Stewing, by the way, is the fancy word for boiling in water until soft when it comes to cooking fruit. The other thing stewed fruit has going for it is you can make up a batch, separate it into containers and freeze it, so that you don't have to do it every day.

These fruits are easy to stew: apples, pears, apricots, plums, nectarines and peaches.

The only ones I worry about peeling are the peaches with the furry skin. I know lots of people peel their apples and pears before they stew them. Whether you peel or not is your choice.

Method:

- Wash the fruit
- Peel the fruit using a knife or a vegetable parer/peeler, optional
- Cut the fruit into pieces, removing stones or cores

- Place the cut pieces of fruit into a saucepan and cover with water
- For apples and pears only - add three or four cloves
- Cover and apply heat
- Turn down the heat when the water starts boiling and let simmer for at least half an hour, longer if you are making a large batch.
- Stir occasionally, so that it doesn't stick to the bottom of the saucepan or dry out because you got distracted and forgot.
- It's cooked when it's soft to the touch with a fork or it tastes great.

When it's cooked, let it cool down before you divide it up for storing in the freezer.

Serving suggestion:

Serve with either yogurt or ice cream.

**Fruit bonus**

Here's a little something you can do with bananas that are starting to look a little tired. Peel a banana and put it in the microwave in a shallow dish, cover and cook for a minute or so. Instant stewed banana!

**Equipment notes**

Stay vigilant. If you get distracted, burnt stewed fruit created by the pot boiling dry not only smells, it also creates a cleaning headache you can do without.

**BBQ**

Barbecues. If there is one type of cooking most men know something about it's barbecuing meat. We love standing around a fire grilling meat and drinking beer, and the women are usually happy to let us do it - provided we don't burn the meat.

A barbecue is great for entertaining but you can also do a barbecue for one, if you'd prefer to keep all those meat or fish cooking smells out of the house.

All you need is a barbecue, a piece of meat or some sausages, some bread and a salad.

In fact, you don't even need the salad. One of the meals we enjoyed as kids was barbecued sausages wrapped in a slice of bread oozing tomato sauce (ketchup). You see people lining up for sausage sizzles all over the place, so I guess I'm not the only one that likes a hot sausage in a piece of bread.

If you can cook it in a frying pan on a cooktop, there's a good chance you can cook it on a barbecue.

The secret to barbecuing meat is the same secret to cooking meat in the house - low to medium heat, patience and the occasional flipping of the meat.

**Equipment notes**

BBQs come in a range of sizes and operating modes. You'd need to be committed to barbecue for one with a heat bead fired Weber Kettle, but any of the gas or electric BBQs are easy to fire up and use. If you clean it each time you use it, a BBQ is easy to maintain. If you don't want to be firing up that four burner, there are a lot of smaller models on the market to choose from.

Like all things mechanical, if you're not sure about how it works read the instructions. And if you can't find the instructions, ask Google.

# SAMPLE MENUS

In this chapter I give you an example of a weekly meals menu or plan. It's a good idea to plan what you're going to eat in advance for two reasons:

- it helps you put some variety into your diet, and
- it makes it easier to compose your shopping list.

**Weekly eating plan**

Day 1

- Breakfast: fruit juice, fruit loaf toast and coffee.
- Lunch: vegetable soup, mineral water and coffee.
- Dinner: pan-fried steak with mixed vegetables, fresh fruit salad with yogurt, mineral water or wine, and coffee.

Day 2

- Breakfast: fruit juice, muesli and yogurt, and coffee.
- Lunch: ham, cheese and tomato sandwich, mineral water and coffee.
- Dinner: pasta with tomato and basil sauce, stewed apples and pears with ice-cream, mineral water or wine, and coffee.

## Day 3

- Breakfast: fruit juice, porridge with banana and yogurt, and coffee.
- Lunch: tuna and mixed green salad, mineral water and coffee.
- Dinner: microwaved salmon, potato and peas, fresh fruit salad with yogurt, mineral water or wine, and coffee.

## Day 4

- Breakfast: fruit juice, two soft boiled eggs and coffee.
- Lunch: pasta with tomato and basils sauce, mineral water and coffee.
- Dinner: beef and vegetable soup with pasta, stewed apples and pears with ice-cream, mineral water or wine, and coffee.

## Day 5

- Breakfast: fruit juice, muesli and yogurt, and coffee.
- Lunch: two sausages with bread, mineral water and coffee.
- Dinner: pan-fried pork chop, rice and mixed vegetables, fresh fruit salad with yogurt, mineral water or wine, and coffee.

## Day 6

- Breakfast: fruit juice, fruit loaf toast and coffee.
- Lunch: salad sandwich, mineral water and coffee.
- Dinner: Thai chicken curry with rice, fresh fruit salad with yogurt, mineral water or wine, and coffee.

## Day 7

- Breakfast: fruit juice, porridge with banana and yogurt, and coffee.
- Lunch: rice and mixed vegetable salad, mineral water and coffee.
- Dinner: pan-fried lamb chop, with mashed potato and mixed vegetables, stewed apples and pears with ice-cream, mineral water or wine, and coffee.

## Observations

There are some common elements in each meal. You've probably noticed I drink a lot of coffee, and that I have listed wine as a possibility for each evening meal. These days I usually drink the mineral water as I like to share a bottle of wine.

When you have your meal plan drawn up, write out your shopping list to make sure you have all the required ingredients. Then it's time to go shopping.

Remember, this is a suggested meal plan for a week based on how I eat. It's here to give you an example of how you can draw up a simple eating plan that only relies on the basic cooking skills described in this book. It doesn't cover all the possible meals you could make using the information in this book. I wanted to leave you some scope for experimenting, and I encourage you to experiment.

# ENTERTAINING

I've included this chapter to illustrate how easy it is to entertain or cook for others.

The secret is to start with a few guests and prepare simple meals, and leave the fancy stuff to the restaurants.

## Eating with friends and family

There are two sorts of entertaining. One is called throwing a party. We have caterers for that.

The other form is eating with friends and family. Start with a small group or one other person.

Once you have mastered a few meals for yourself, it doesn't take much imagination to turn a meal for one into a meal for two or more.

I started entertaining with stews and curries, and fruit salad with ice-cream.

One of the easiest meals to prepare for a small group is pasta. Use the whole packet in a large saucepan, buy a big jar of pasta sauce and a fresh container of grated cheese. A packet of pasta will make enough pasta for four people. If they're big eaters use two packets. It doesn't cost a fortune.

Another easy meal for sharing is frozen vegetable and beef soup with pasta. Cook up the recipe and use the lot. Add a cup of pasta for each guest into the mix. A roast is another good entertainment meal for a small group of friends or that special person in your life.

Remember, you can always serve two or more dishes. For example, start with a small bowl of pasta for each guest, followed by pan-fried steak with mixed vegetables, and then fresh fruit salad and ice-cream.

And don't forget the barbecue for entertaining. You need to be organised if you're doing all the preparation. The secret is to prepare your salads before the guests arrive and to cook the meat when they're enjoying their first round of drinks. You can also offer to provide the meat and ask your friends to bring a salad. People love to help, so ask them.

**Equipment notes**

The most important aspect of entertaining is ambience or atmosphere. What this means is thinking about setting the scene for the meal you are planning to share.

For family and friends this might mean giving the place a clean and putting a few things away. Remember to clean the bathroom and the toilet, and to put out a fresh hand towel. When you're setting the table, use a table cloth and put out some paper serviettes.

If you're entertaining a special friend, doing all of the above and adding a flower and a couple of small candles to the table setting, sends the signal that you have put some thought into preparing for the evening together.

## OVER TO YOU

Cooking4One is a list of instructions or suggestions for preparing a range of meals. It's up to you to turn these words into something edible at your place. My hope is that I have successfully encouraged you to give cooking for yourself a go.

I hope you get the same sense of achievement I felt when I first realized I could cook more than a piece of toast. It's really satisfying knowing you can feed yourself, and if you're going to be on your own for some time, or maybe for the rest of your life, being able to feed yourself is an essential life skill.

Food shopping is always interesting, if you take the time to look around. Every time I go to the supermarket I discover something else I could try. This is one reason why I always take a list but I do allow myself to buy a few things that aren't on the list - in the spirit of experimentation.

When you first start out you might be pointing to what you want in the butchers but don't let that put you off. They'll tell you what's it's called. In a lot of places these days they cater for novice shoppers - with little signs telling you what everything is.

Remember, they want you to come back so they're usually happy to answer your questions.

Cooking is fun when you know how to do it. The secret to getting to that knowing how to do it spot is practice. You've no doubt heard all the buzz around 10,000 hours of practice turning anybody with a bit of skill and a sense of dedication into a master practitioner. It won't take you that long but you do have to apply the knowledge in this book if you want to eat the outcome.

Bon appétit!

# SANITY SAVERS

# INTRODUCTION

Being on your own, following the end of a long-term relationship, can be quite daunting. It often presents challenges, like boredom and loneliness.

In this section, my intention is to introduce you to some strategies that will help you keep your sanity intact.

In what follows, I share seven strategies for finding constructive or interesting ways to use your alone time, and two personal growth and development strategies you can use to stay connected with the world, and to explore some of life's more intriguing questions.

These strategies will remind you that there are things you can do, things you can learn, places you can visit, and friends you can make. They also highlight the value of making commitments to your personal growth and engaging with others.

Over the last several years I have spent a fair amount of time on my own. My long-term relationship may not have ended when my wife accepted a position in another country, but it certainly changed form.

*Introduction*

Since finding myself on my own for months at a time, I have employed the strategies I am sharing with you to write several books, focus on my spiritual journey, establish a blog, and stay connected to my extended family. I've also acquired a set of new skills, related to self-publishing and online marketing, had a lot of fun, met some interesting people, and travelled.

To be honest, I haven't had the time to feel bored or lonely.

I recommend that you explore some of the activities suggested in the first seven strategies. Discover which ones work for you and make the most of what they have to offer.

I encourage you to embrace strategies eight and nine: staying connected and befriending yourself. I believe these are essential for the ongoing sanity of anyone living alone.

# READING

You're reading this book, so I guess it's safe to assume you already know something about the value of reading. I know a lot of guys who read the paper, well at least the sports pages, and think that's all there is to reading. We're going a bit further than that.

In my experience, reading is one of the more enjoyable pastimes for someone living alone. It's not expensive, it can be done almost anywhere, and it's more active and engaging than watching TV, which the neuroscientists describe as a passive activity. If you want to keep your brain active and increase your chances of not getting dementia, reading is a better choice than TV, simply because you need to use active imagination when you read. If you're not quite sure what that means, consider that what you see on the TV is always someone else's visual interpretation of the story - whether you're watching the history channel or the news. When you're reading the story in words, you get to dream up your own visual interpretation or mental pictures of the words, based on your unique perspective of the world. That's the bit that exercises your brain cells.

Reading is an activity that can be done for several different reasons, which we'll explore in the following sections.

**Reading for entertainment**

This is the world of fiction or storytelling. There is an ever-increasing supply of stories for you to choose from, so you'll never run out of books to read. There are books for every imaginable interest.

Go to any brick and mortar or online bookstore and just look at the list of categories. Okay, you might not be into romance or erotica or that vampire paranormal stuff, but there are stacks of other categories to choose from: crime, mysteries, thrillers, action-hero, espionage, historical-fiction, fantasy, science-fiction, war stories and literary masterpieces to name a few. And, they all have sub-genres or sub-categories with thousands of authors to choose from.

I'd also include biographies and autobiographies in this section, not that I am suggesting that they are works of fiction, but because we read them more for their entertainment value than for any other reason - a form of voyeurism.

If you haven't ventured beyond the papers or the self-help section in recent years, do yourself a favour, and buy yourself a novel, or go to your local library and borrow one or two.

If you need a place to start, try one of my Inspector West novels, a Chief Inspector Gamache novel by Louise Penny, or a Roy Grace novel by Peter James.

## Reading for information

Another reason to read is to find information. This is the world of non-fiction, where you can go to get help or find out about those things that interest you. This book is in this category.

This is where you find the history books and the how-to books, shelved with the cooking books and the art and craft books, along with all the political science and real science books.

There is some fascinating material to be found in this part of the library or bookstore. If you want to know something about Islam or Buddhism or Christianity, or the history of warfare, or how they get the retina display on an iPad, or to discover who was behind the global financial crisis, this is the place. There will be a book here for you, no matter what you're interested in.

This is also the place to find information on setting up a business, money management, along with ideas on time management and all sorts of ways you can be more productive. It's also where you'll find all those 'how-to-get-rich-quick' books, which seem to be multiplying like rabbits after a good rain.

Despite the danger, this is one of my favourite parts of the bookstore. This is where you can find thought-provoking books like: *The Black Swan* by Nassin Nicholas Taleb; *The Master Strategist* by Ketan J Patel; and *Hot, Flat and Crowded* by Thomas L Friedmann.

## Reading for inspiration

Sometimes, you simply need a lift. Fortunately, there are books that can help you get through it when you're down.

When you're pondering the meaning of life, or wondering why you're here, and what you're supposed to be doing with yourself, there are books to help with that too.

The thing to remember is that you are not alone on the planet, even if you are alone at home. There are others who are treading the same path or who have gone before you, and some of them have written about their experiences and what they learnt along the way.

We like to think that we have original ideas, unique questions or personal moments that no-one else could possibly understand. But when we engage with fellow pilgrims, we discover that we were mistaken in our belief.

When I was much younger, I started in this part of the bookstore with Wayne Dyer, before moving on to Richard Rohr, Osho, John O'Donohue, Deepak Chopra and Paul Ferrini, to name a few of the authors in this part of my library.

In 2014 I added my own contribution to this library - *Sharing the Journey: Reflections of a Reluctant Mystic*.

**Format: books, e-books and blogs**

Once upon a time, we were restricted to reading paper based books, magazines, comics and newspapers. You can still read the paper version, but now you can choose an electronic version for many titles.

The advent of the e-book, in particular, has changed the reading experience for anyone with an e-reader device, tablet computer or smartphone. Not only are e-books a lot cheaper to buy, you don't have to worry about having the shelf space to store them either. Amazon, Apple or Kobo, or any of the other online stores, will store them in the cloud for you, to access from anywhere at any time and, of course, you can store a copy on your device to read without having to be online.

I do most of my reading these days on my iPad, even the books I buy from Amazon or Kobo. All you need is the app for your device. I have a couple of Kindles, one from my pre-iPad days and a newer Kindle Paper White, that was a gift, so even when the iPad is recharging I still have a device to read on, and they all seem to know which page I'm up to, provided I turn them on within range of a wireless router.

Despite having all those e-readers, there are still times when I like to read paper based books. There is something about that experience you just don't get with an e-book. Besides, I have a library with a few thousand printed titles that I like to revisit. There is something about sitting in a room full of books that you just can't capture with an electronic library of hundreds of titles stored in the cloud, or on that device in your hand.

On the other hand, if you're someone who changes apartments frequently or who travels, an e-book based library makes a lot of sense. Another thing I like about e-books is that if I see a book I want to read at two am in the morning, I can buy it on the spot and start reading without leaving my chair. It can take up to two or three weeks for a paperback to arrive in Australia from Amazon or the Book Depository, and there aren't any local bookshops open at that hour where I live.

The electronic world has also brought us the world of blogging, which provides online magazines or journals written by people like you and me, on any topic you can think of, which you can read for free if you have internet access. You can find a blog on any topic simply by asking Google or any other search engine for: 'your topic' blogs.

Blogs provide readers with an opportunity to interact with writers. If you want to say something about the content of a blog post or article, you simply add a comment. If you find a blog you really enjoy, you can sign up to have the content delivered to your email inbox.

Just reading through the stream of comments is often as much fun as reading the blog post itself.

**The online library**

If you want to do some study, there are hundreds of courses available online.

Check out openculture.com for details on some of the more serious university offerings.

Fortunately, there are other options for those of us who are just interested in finding out about stuff. We can turn to YouTube and Vimeo, two places with lots of video presentations on a range of interesting topics.

If you're interested in short, thought-provoking presentations, try Ted talks.

If you prefer PowerPoint presentations, check out what's available on SlideShare.net.

If you don't mind paying a few dollars for a course, see what interests you over at Udemy.com.

There is something else you can do in the online library that they don't encourage in your local library: you can discuss books with other readers. One place you can do this is at Goodreads.com, which allows you to join groups based on interest or book categories, where you will find other readers discussing the books.

**Resources**

**Online courses**

Open Culture - www.openculture.com

Udemy - www.udemy.com

## Online presentations

Ted Talks - www.ted.com/talks

YouTube - www.youtube.com

Vimeo - www.vimeo.com

SlideShare - www.slideshare.net

## Online book clubs

GoodReads - www.goodreads.com

# WRITING

Not everybody wants to write a book; yet many of us dream about doing just that. Obviously, writing a book is one of the options I elected to pursue to help me pass the time when I am alone. If you're interested in how that works, you can read about it below.

Writing a book is not the only writing option. There are several other forms of writing you can pursue for pleasure or self-discovery. In this section, we'll explore some of the ways you can use writing as a pastime.

**Writing a book**

Prior to 2008, when the Kindle hit the market, writing and publishing a book was a daunting task. Not only did you have to write the book, you had to find someone willing to publish it, unless you were prepared to pay thousands of dollars for an initial print run, and then spend your spare time trying to get people to buy the 3,000 copies you had in the garage, backroom or trunk of your car.

Today, with e-books and print-on-demand technology, it's a lot easier to get a book into circulation. You still have to write, edit, format, proofread and design a cover (or get a team of people to do those things for you) to produce a book, but it no longer costs a small fortune to publish one.

You can spend a lot of time writing a book. A book like this one, for example, takes around thirty days to write, if you've got two hours a night to devote to writing, and you apply yourself to the task. It takes another thirty days or so to polish your first draft into a book you can publish.

A 90,000-word novel, like those in my Inspector West series, takes considerably longer to write. It takes me around six months to write the first draft, at around 700 to 1,000 words a day. It generally takes another three months to complete the first round of revisions and edits, before I hand the manuscript over to one of my beta-readers for feedback.

That's usually followed by another couple of months of editing, formatting and proofreading before the novel is ready for publishing.

The whole process of self-publishing and marketing your books is an interesting and time-consuming field in itself. In fact, there is a whole library of books you can read on that subject. There is also a worldwide community of Indie or self-published authors out there you can tap into for help.

One other thing to consider, if you decide to write a book or two, is getting the right writing software. You can do a lot with Microsoft Word or any other word processing application, but you can do a lot more with a dedicated writing application like Scrivener.

And, of course, you can write a book for yourself. There is no rule that says you have to publish what you write.

## Blogging

Blogging is another recent development in the world of writing.

Blogging is a way of writing and publishing articles or opinion pieces, sharing insights, or asking questions. You can think of blogging as a way of producing your own online magazine.

Maybe words are not your thing. Blogging also gives you the opportunity to share your digital photographs or artwork. It's also a way of engaging with the people who find your content.

One of the great things about blogging is that it can be done for free.

Anyone with an internet connection and an email address can set up a free WordPress blog. Just go to WordPress.com and get started. They have plenty of resources to help first-time bloggers. How do you think I got started?

You can check out my blog at www.petermulraney.com.

One thing I can tell you about blogging, apart from it being a lot of fun, is that it takes time, which is why we are discussing it here.

## Courses and presentations

Perhaps you have technical or other knowledge you can share. Instead of taking a course at a place like Udemy.com, you could offer one. Or you could share your knowledge by uploading videos to sites like YouTube or Vimeo, or PowerPoint presentations to share on SlideShare.

Note: all these sites have Terms and Conditions describing what you can and cannot do on them. There is some pretty easy-to-use software available for making simple videos, like VideoScribe or

Vidra, which I used to create the book trailers for the books in this series, on my iPad.

## Journals

There is some writing that is best done with pen and paper. This is where journals come in. A journal is a book you create by writing down your thoughts, and your answers to those questions that bother you, or that you have been putting off looking at for years.

Journals are a pathway to self-discovery or self-recovery, which we'll cover more comprehensively in chapter 9. You can write what you like in a journal. You're the only person who is likely to ever read it, and you'll be dead when, and if, anybody else reads it, unless you come from New York, where everybody seems to publish a book about their personal journey.

You can use any sort of notebook for journal work. I prefer the ones with lined pages but, if you're more artistic, you might prefer a notebook with blank pages or a visual journal, which you can buy from places that sell art supplies. And, remember, you're the only person who needs to be able to read it. Often, it's the act of writing that does the work, and maybe you'll never reread what you write. There are plenty of pages in my journals I have trouble reading, so heaven help anyone who stumbles across them when I'm gone.

If you're not sure how to get started, purchase journals with a daily question, reflection or a theme, like a gratitude journal, where you buy books or from one of the many online sites that support journaling.

You can also use a journal to record your insights and responses to questions and exercises you find in self-development or personal growth books.

I promise you'll learn more about life and yourself from journaling than you ever will watching TV.

## Diaries

A diary is a specific type of journal used for recording the events of your day. In a diary you simply create a record of what happened. Once you cross the line into reflecting on what happened, or why certain events occurred in the course of your journey, you've crossed over into creating a journal or the work of self-discovery. There is nothing wrong with that. Moving from diary to journal is actually quite common.

## Letter writing

If blogging, which is like writing a letter to the world, is not your cup of tea, maybe old style letter writing is something you can revisit. We may live in a world of instant communication but people still appreciate the thought you put into a handwritten letter.

Although letter writing seems to have become a dying art-form, thanks to email and, more recently, social media, it still has it's place.

I notice that people still write letters to the editor. You could do that if you're into reading the paper. You could make that a weekly or daily activity if you're seriously into current affairs, although be warned, a lot of that is done by email these days.

Then there are all those people in your life that perhaps you haven't seen in a while, who might appreciate a letter or a card letting them know that you're thinking about them. Postage is still inexpensive, which is one reason why the postal services are going broke.

If you're feeling civic, maybe you could send your local politician a few ideas or join a letter writing campaign to raise awareness of issues in your local community.

**Resources**

**Blogging**

WordPress - www.wordpress.com

My WordPress blog - www.petermulraney.com

**Journals with prompts to get you started**

Soulful Journals - www.soulfuljournals.com

**Video making tools**

VideoScribe - www.videoscribe.co

Vidra for iPad - www.tentouchapps.com/vidra

## LEARNING A NEW SKILL

How often have you said that you'd like to do something if you had the time?

Well, now that you have the time, what's holding you back?

Or maybe there is something you liked doing as a boy that you put aside in order to cope with life's responsibilities. Might be worth revisiting that interest, instead of sitting on the couch watching TV or drowning your sorrows with your poison of choice.

**Musical instruments**

I have a guitar in one corner of my studio from a long ago time when I thought I might learn to play it. Maybe you have an instrument hidden somewhere at your place, or sitting in plain sight, if it's a piano, that you learnt to play as a child but haven't touched in years. One of the benefits of being on your own is there is no-one to complain about the noise as you reacquaint yourself with that instrument, even if that instrument is your voice.

If you've never learnt to play an instrument or to sing, one comment from the guy who patiently helped me learn a few chords, all those years ago, that has stayed with me is this: the best students are old people and little kids, because they're willing to have a go, and they don't care if they make fools of themselves in the process. So, if you have reached that age where you can let go and relax, maybe this is something for you.

If you have an instrument and simply need to tune up your skills, the Garage Band app for the iPad or iMac might be all you need to get playing again. I'm sure they have similar apps for all those Android devices out there.

If you're new to the world of music, you'll need to seek out tuition at your local community college or find a private tutor, and pay for lessons. Not everything in life is free.

Learning to play an instrument takes hours of practice on a daily basis. And, when you get good at it, as you will with all that practice, you can enjoy the beautiful music.

Now, there's a way to fill in all those lonely hours.

**Foreign languages**

Did you learn a foreign language at school?

Okay, so some of us are old enough to confess to studying Latin. Unfortunately, there aren't too many places where you can either brush up or converse in that language these days, unless you have a job in the Vatican. I guess there could be some lonely guys there looking for conversation partners.

There are lots of other languages. In my case, I studied Italian after meeting the Italian girl that became my wife.

Knowing a second language opens up some interesting travel opportunities, and allows you to gain an appreciation of how people from other cultures see the world.

If you live in America, can you speak and read Spanish?

By my reckoning, Spanish is the second language in the USA. Everywhere I walk around New York, for example, I hear it and see it written on signs, even those belonging to the New York City Council on construction sites. Why not become part of the bilingual population?

European languages are probably the easiest for native English speakers to learn, as they use the same alphabet, but you could challenge yourself with something more exotic like Mandarin, Japanese, Russian, Greek or Arabic, which use different alphabets.

One of my sons, for example, is learning Japanese, where they draw on three alphabets for the written form of the language. Fortunately, they teach it phonetically to English speakers, using words written with letters from the English alphabet. Mind you, he has an app on his smartphone for working out how to draw the kanji or characters.

Learning a language is something best done in groups, where you can practise conversing in the language, exchanging letters, watching films or reading to each other from books and newspapers. Again, check out your local community college, or ask your search engine of choice where you can learn to speak the language that interests you in your part of the world. You can also go it alone, with one of the many on-line courses or podcasts devoted to teaching foreign languages.

If you really want to become proficient, there is nothing like total immersion or going to learn the language in country.

No matter how you do it, learning a foreign language can fill up your hours and introduce you to other people with a similar interest.

Who knows, you might even make some new friends in a foreign country.

## Woodwork and other practical stuff

A lot of us like doing things with our hands. If you haven't played in this space for a while, there are places you can go to revitalise your skills or learn new ones.

One such place goes under the name of Men's Sheds, a movement that evolved from a community based initiative to address men's social and health issues, which kicked off in Australia in the 1990s, into an expanding worldwide movement. Men's Sheds are places where men gather, support each other, and develop and practise practical skills.

In Australia, where most people still live in houses and not apartments, a lot of men have a backyard shed, where they tinker with stuff or build things. I do most of my writing in my shed. Mind you, it's a far cry from the humble backyard shed of my father's generation. I might refer to it as 'the shed', after-all, it started life as a galvanised iron, two car garage, but when my sons were filling up the driveway with their cars, I built a carport and had the shed renovated - read insulated, air conditioned, lined, glass windows and sliding doors, and tiles on the floor. These days it looks more like a library than a shed. I understand it would be referred to as a man cave, in some other parts of the world.

Woodworking isn't the only thing you can do in a shed. There is a whole range of crafts you can enjoy from kite building, to scrapbooking, to paper making, to blacksmithing, and things like quilting and knitting. That's right, you don't have to restrict yourself to the traditional men's crafts. Of course, you can do all those other manly mechanical things like restoring cars and building boats, if that's what you're interested in exploring.

## Creative crafts

If the functional crafts aren't your thing, what about the creative?

In my shed I have two desks. There is the digital desk, where I write and do things on my iMac, and there is the analogue desk, where my art materials reside. At the art desk I doodle, sketch, splash watercolours, work in acrylics, and do calligraphy. I did a lot of portraits, in several media, the year my wife went to New York. It helped to fill the gap.

Art is a lot of fun, and you don't have to show or sell your work. I've completed a few calligraphic pieces on commission for friends, but most of my artwork has never left the shed. Some people do all their work in sketchbooks.

If you don't think you can draw or paint, there is a wide choice of inexpensive apps you can download for generating digital art. I've got some of them, too. The logo on the front cover of this book, for example, came from one of those apps, and I sometimes use those apps to generate the images I post on my blog.

Digital photography is another activity you can spend hours with. If you have a smartphone, you've always got a camera in your pocket, and there are some fun apps for playing with your photos. One of the apps I like is Comic Life 3, which allows you to add comments and other effects to your photos, and to compile them into comics for sharing with your friends. Comic Life 3 is so easy to use that primary school kids, in classrooms all over the world, are using it for storyboarding.

If you really want to get into editing your photos there's always Photoshop, if you don't mind spending a few dollars.

Like everything else, there is an online community of artists offering free and subscription services to help you learn how to do almost anything artistic. A lot of the free material is on YouTube.

Two art sites I use for inspiration and know-how are FivePencilMethod and ArtTutor.

**Resources**

**Art**

Five Pencil Method - www.fivepencilmethod.com

Art Tutor - www.arttutor.com

**Crafts**

Madman knitting blog - www.madmanknitting.wordpress.com

**Men's Sheds**

Australian Men's Sheds Association - www.mensshed.org

Men's Sheds UK - www.menssheds.org.uk

# EXERCISING

There are many reasons for exercising, most of them related to fitness and wellbeing but, in our context, exercise is one of those activities you can devote time to on a regular basis.

Taken seriously, exercise can consume hours of your time, but there is no need to take it to those levels, at least initially. Not everyone is destined to be an Olympic Athlete or a Masters' Champion.

Anyone can exercise. Some forms are easy and inexpensive, and everyone benefits from regular exercise.

If you haven't exercised for a while, you might want to check with your doctor before you take on anything strenuous. Another word of warning before you begin, start slowly and gradually increase your work rate over time.

Rushing into exercise, of any type, with enthusiasm is a painful experience for the muscles, and results in a lot of people giving up before they really begin.

## Walking, jogging and skipping

You know how to walk but, if you're like the rest of us, you've been driving the car, catching the subway and taking the elevator. That's okay. I do those things, too.

A gentle way of easing yourself into walking is to put on some loose-fitting clothes and your sneakers, or any other soft-soled shoes, and go for a ten to twenty minute walk in the evening, or morning if you're an early riser.

If you live near a park or a river, they are great places to walk. If you don't, go for a walk around the block, or up and down the street, and see what's going on in your neighbourhood from street level.

If you find that walking isn't exciting enough, get some decent cross-trainers or running shoes and start jogging. This one requires a bit more commitment, at least three times a week, but daily is even better. I was a runner in my youth but I confess to slowing down - now I walk.

Walking and jogging are two activities that lend themselves to being done in groups. Exercising with a friend or two is a way to make it a habit, and it gives you an opportunity to talk as you exercise together.

Sometimes the weather is against you when it comes to either walking or jogging. This is where skipping comes in. All you need is a skipping rope and a space to turn it. Skipping might be a simple exercise, but as with all the others, show it some respect and work your way into it gradually, otherwise you will end up sore. Skipping is a bit like jogging on the spot, and it's good for the abs too - all that shaking up and down tightens those belly muscles.

## Swimming

If you want to give your body a bit more of a total workout, consider swimming. Don't know how to swim? They teach adults. Look up adult swimming classes in your local area with Google or any other search engine.

This is another form of exercise that takes time. When you get into swimming laps to increase your fitness, you can easily spend an hour at the pool. Swimming is a fairly solitary pursuit, unless you join a club. There are social and competitive swimming clubs. Ask at your local pool.

## Cycling

There are several levels at which you can tackle cycling, and there is a large range of cycles or bikes available to choose from. See the Wikipedia link in resources for more details.

For our purposes, we'll consider stationary cycles and road bikes.

Stationary cycles are the exercise machines you generally find in gyms, which you can also buy for home use if you don't have access to a gym, or don't want to join one. A stationary or exercise bike gives you all the exercise without any of the dangers of riding on the road, or any of the worries about riding in rain or heat.

Road bikes are designed for riding on urban streets and dedicated cycle or bike paths. This is the type you are probably familiar with, from either your childhood or from having kids.

As with walking or jogging, cycling is an activity that you can either do alone or in groups. You've no doubt seen groups of cyclists on the roads, and sitting in or around coffee shops. From my observations, cycling seems to be a weekend activity for many people.

In fact, you can join touring groups that go for day or weekend tours of the countryside. Joining such groups allows you to make new friends and fill up a whole day or weekend having fun, instead of sitting home navel gazing, and wondering what to do with yourself. You can even go on bike tours in other parts of the country or in overseas locations. Imagine yourself spending hours training and then enjoying a whole week, or longer, exploring another place with a group of like-minded people.

This is another activity you'll need to spend money on if you don't own a bike. You don't have to buy a top of the range carbon fibre bike for thousands of dollars. You can still get a serviceable bike for a few hundred dollars, or less, if you go for a used bike from your local cycling store, or from eBay or similar sites.

You can always trade up later, if you fall in love with cycling, and that's when you can think about the lycra and the fancy shoes. Until then, you can comfortably cycle in street clothes and sneakers. You see people doing that all the time. There's even a lad in my neighbourhood that flies past me on his bike wearing a suit, when I'm walking to the bus stop on my way to the office.

If your bike hasn't been used for a while, like years, it will probably need new tyres and a service before you take it out on the road.

Bicycle maintenance is another skill you can spend time mastering along the way.

**Yoga and Pilates**

These are exercises you can do indoors with a minimum of equipment. The basic requirement is an exercise mat and some loose-fitting clothes. No special shoes required, you can do these exercises barefoot.

It's probably best to go to classes to learn how to do either of these, but you can teach yourself the basic moves using DVD or on-line courses, or an instruction book. The advantage of starting by going to classes is the commitment required to establish the exercise habit. Use Google or any other search engine to find out what's available in your area.

Don't be fooled by the apparent ease of either of these exercise regimes. Some of the exercises can be pretty strenuous, and many require a lot of practice before you'll feel comfortable doing them.

Once you get a basic routine under your belt, you can easily spend thirty minutes to an hour each day on these exercises.

Pilates is still on my list of things to start. I've got the book and the exercise mat.

**The gym**

Recently, I listened to a discussion on gym membership on WYNC, my favourite New York radio station, which was exploring the monthly subscription business model used in the industry. Most people sign up, pay monthly and don't go. So a word of warning. Don't sign up unless you know you will actually go. You will be better off paying the casual rate, until you're in a position to make an informed decision based on your actual attendance. Keep a written record to establish your attendance pattern. Apparently, most people lie to themselves about how often they go to the gym once they have signed up.

If you're looking to work with a personal trainer or work with weights, the gym is the place to go. If you're simply looking to increase your general level of fitness, without getting seriously into weights, you could consider setting up a gym at home. There are a lot of exercises you can do using your body weight. Simply look up that topic with Google or your search engine of choice, or check the link below in resources. If you live in an apartment building with a gym, that you already pay for in your rent, you already have a home gym. All you have to do is use it.

## Sleeping

Activity is one side of the exercise coin. The other is sleeping.

Most of us know that we turn into grumpy old men if we don't get sufficient sleep. There is no need to deny yourself sleep just because you'll be sleeping on your own. So instead of staying up late watching TV, go to bed and get a good night's sleep.

Not only will a lack of sleep make you grumpy, there's plenty of evidence (which you can read online if you need to convince yourself - ask our friend Google about sleep deprivation) that not getting enough sleep leads to things like:

- Reduced alertness
- Shortened attention span
- Slower than normal reaction time
- Poor judgement
- Reduced awareness of the environment and situation
- Reduced decision-making skills
- Poor memory
- Reduced concentration
- Increased likelihood of mentally 'stalling' or fixating on one thought
- Increased likelihood of moodiness and bad temper
- Reduced work efficiency
- Loss of motivation

- Errors of omission – making a mistake by forgetting to do something
- Errors of commission – making a mistake by doing something, but choosing the wrong option
- Micro-sleep – brief periods of involuntary sleeping that range from a few seconds to a few minutes in duration.

I got this list from an article on sleep Google found for me at betterhealth.vic.gov.au.

**Some reminders**

Something you might want to consider while we're discussing looking after your body - it's designed to run on water, not alcohol.

I'm not saying you shouldn't drink, but I am reminding you that you need to put some water into the system - daily.

I'm a practitioner of the middle way - I drink alcohol in moderation, I do some exercise, I'm conscious of the portion size of meals, and I get a good night's sleep.

She might not be there nagging you to watch what you eat, to limit the amount of booze you drink, and to get out there and get some exercise. But that is not a good reason for not looking after yourself.

And remember, you're the one in charge of your physical wellbeing, so if you feel sick or off color, don't wait until you can't get out of bed. Go see a doctor or a medical practitioner of whatever persuasion you're attracted to.

There's no-one to impress with 'soldiering on' when you're living on your own.

## Resources

### Bikes

Types of bicycles - www.wikipedia.org/wiki/List_of_bicycle_types

### Yoga and Pilates

Wikihow-Yoga for beginners - www.wikihow.com/Do-Yoga-for-Absolute-Beginners
Wikihow-Categories of Pilates - www.wikihow.com/Category:Pilates

### Body weight exercises

50 body weight exercises you can do anywhere - www.greatist.com/fitness/50-bodyweight-exercises-you-can-do-anywhere

## GROWING THINGS

I'll start with a confession. I live in a suburban house with both a front and back garden. Quite a few of the images on my blog are photographs of plants in those gardens. But, to be honest, although I enjoy gardening, I have a gardener, who spends a couple of hours every second week maintaining them. I also live in a part of the world where it does not snow, so we can enjoy our gardens year round, provided we can keep up the watering required to help the plants get through the hot, dry Australian summer - and, fortunately, someone invented automated irrigation systems to take care of that.

A few of my neighbours, who do not have gardeners, spend most of their weekends in their gardens. A garden is a place where you can either spend hours working in it or a place where you can spend hours enjoying doing some of the other activities I've mentioned, like reading, drawing, painting, photography, exercise or simply meditating.

Gardening may not take up a lot of your time, but it's an activity you can include in your daily or weekly schedule, along with whatever else you choose to do to enjoy your hours with yourself.

## Herbs, vegetables and flowers

My current gardens are in the category referred to as aesthetic. I have a couple of fruit trees and grow a few herbs, in pots, but most of the plant life is there for looking at.

Some of my friends have extensive vegetable gardens - one of the side benefits of being connected to an Italian community.

If you have the space, you can grow a lot of your own fruit and vegetables, or like one of my older, retired friends, with an extensive and productive garden, you can supply your family and friends, especially over the summer.

If you live in the suburbs, you can do more than mow the grass every week or so.

## The indoor garden

Gardening is not restricted to the outdoors in temperate climates. You can also become an indoor gardener, using pot plants or hydroponics to grow a range of vegetables. Many of the vegetables you buy at the supermarket these days are grown using hydroponics.

You can find out how it all works by asking Google or any other search engine, or by following the link to what Wikipedia has on the topic in the resources section below.

Start with a few pots or a small hydroponics kit, unless you're intending to convert your shed into an urban farm.

## Community gardens

Another way of getting into gardening is to become part of a community garden.

A community garden generally involves a group of people growing things on a shared piece of land. In some parts of the world, this may involve establishing a garden on an abandoned allotment. In other places, City Councils or individuals make a piece of land available for people living in a neighbourhood to grow food.

You can find a community garden in your area using your favourite search engine, or you can start one. Either way, you'll get to meet people and spend time out of the house.

For more details, follow the link to the Wikipedia article on community gardens in the resources section.

## Taking care of public spaces

If you're not into growing things, there is one other 'gardening' option you can consider, which I understand is popular with people in some parts of the world: taking care of public spaces. Query your search engine on that topic, to see what other people are doing around the world to take care of their public spaces.

On a local level, this can simply mean adopting a street or part of a park, for example, and spending a few hours each week removing litter. You get to spend a few hours doing something and the world is left a better place that day. And you never know, if others see you cleaning up your adopted space they might even stop littering, because they know someone cares about the place. They even have a name for this approach to public engagement - the broken windows theory.

Another thing to keep in mind about public gardens is that they are microcosms of nature, places you can go to recharge your spirit.

**Resources**

Hydroponics - www.wikipedia.org/wiki/Hydroponics

Community Gardening - www.wikipedia.org/wiki/Community_gardening

# SERVING

Looking after public spaces is one example of the many ways you can serve your community.

One of the best things about serving others is, while you're doing it, you're not thinking about yourself or how lonely you feel. It's a great way to vary your routine and give yourself a lift at the same time. Additionally, you get to meet people and make new friends.

**Service clubs**

These are groups of people who volunteer their time to help others. Rotary and Lions are two of the better-known service clubs in the English speaking world, but there are lots of others.

Many of these clubs hold weekly meetings, some do weekend events, and most sponsor some mission or cause; so they are always holding fund-raising events that you can get involved in.

Ask your search engine of choice about service clubs in your local area, or seek out members of a service club you know about, and find out how you can participate. An easy way to start is to attend some events being held by clubs in your area, and asking a few questions.

## Sporting clubs

Amateur sporting clubs are always looking for administrative and team support staff. If your kids, or grandkids, play a sport you can do more than just attend the game. Kids' basketball teams, for example, are always looking for someone to score.

If you played a sport in your youth, consider becoming a referee for a junior league or local competition. You'll probably need to do a refresher or training course, and you might need to increase your fitness level, but you'd be making a contribution that allows the kids to play.

If you don't feel up to making that sort of commitment, consider adopting a local team, and at least go along to the games and cheer the kids on - everyone likes an audience. Even that level of participation is better than staying home alone feeling lost and bored.

## Charities

Most communities have charity or church groups that rely on volunteers to run soup kitchens and shelters for the homeless, or to support families in need. Some of these groups are religious based, for example, the St Vincent de Paul Society or the Salvation Army, but there are many secular organisations as well, like Meals on Wheels, for example, which delivers food to homebound and elderly people, that you can look into joining. And let's face it, these days, no-one is going to reject your service based on your religious persuasion if you volunteer to help out.

## Local community

Another option for spending some time in service is volunteering to do things for people in your local community. Perhaps you could read to people in the local aged-care facility or simply visit an older person to chat.

Are there people in your street or building that need help with their shopping, cleaning or some other task, like getting to an appointment? Not everyone can afford to hire help, and not everyone is ordering home delivery online. Some don't know how. Maybe you can show them how it's done or do it for them.

You could volunteer to participate in any senior citizen service programs provided by your local City Council. In my area, for example, they are always looking for someone to drive the community bus or join the graffiti removal squad. Or, instead of caring for public spaces on your own, join a local land-care or conservation group.

All or any of these options will get you out of the house and mixing with other people.

## Family

Another group you can serve is your family, especially if they live in the same town or city. Some family time will be social, but there will be times when family members appreciate a helping hand. If you have grandchildren, offer to be the babysitter while the young parents have a night out or go away for the weekend. If you like gardening, maybe you can be the gardener your kids, brother, sister or parents, can't afford.

Maybe you don't need to visit an aged care facility to spend time with a lonely older person - you could simply spend some time with your parents or widowed mother. If they live out of town, consider getting them onto to Skype or a similar service. If my 85 year old mother can use it, yours probably can too, and you can spend time chatting and seeing how they are, instead of watching TV.

**Resources**

**Service clubs**

Rotary International - www.wikipedia.org/wiki/Rotary_International
Lions Clubs International - www.wikipedia.org/wiki/Lions_Clubs_International
Kiwanis International - www.wikipedia.org/wiki/Kiwanis

**Charities**

Society of St Vincent De Paul - www.wikipedia.org/wiki/Society_of_Saint_Vincent_de_Paul
Meals on Wheels - www.wikipedia.org/wiki/Meals_on_Wheels

**Online communication service for connecting family members**

Skype - www.skype.com/en/

# HAVING FUN

If you're not inclined to service or learning new skills, at least resolve to have some fun.

Being on your own, you don't need to worry about what anybody else considers to be fun or entertainment either - you get to please yourself.

It's okay to indulge yourself every now and then. It's certainly better than sitting home and feeling miserable.

**Going to the movies**

Stay home and watch it on the small screen or venture out and watch it on the big screen, with surround sound, at the local cinema complex. You know it will be a different experience, and who knows whom you might bump into while you're there. Why stay home every night of the week?

You don't have to restrict yourself to the movies. There's live theatre, opera and the ballet to experience, especially if you've never been.

Remember those live music shows from your youth? They still have them. It might cost a bit more but, hey, what the heck? It's your money.

Not happening in your town? Make a weekend of it and fly over to wherever it's on, or take yourself for a drive and see some of the country as well.

**Eating out - treat yourself**

Hopefully, you've taken my advice in Cooking4One and learnt to cook for yourself. That doesn't mean you have to eat home alone every night though.

It might not be much fun eating alone in a restaurant on Valentine's Day, but there are 364 other days to choose from. More and more restaurants are catering for solo diners, but who says you have to eat alone? Ask a friend along.

If you're sitting at home all day, every day, a change of scenery for your midday or evening meal might be just the trick for brightening up your day.

Consider combining eating out with another event, like visiting the barber, assuming you still have enough hair to make that worthwhile, or going to a movie, so that you maximise the time you're spending out of the house.

If you're still gainfully or otherwise employed, consider eating out on the way home, or go to a movie first and then eat with the nine o'clock crowd, before going home.

**Travel**

They claim that a change is as good as a holiday. Well, let me tell you that a holiday beats a change - every time.

If you have the funds, overseas travel is worth the effort. If you don't have a lot of money, travel locally. My mother, for example, goes on what we boys refer to as 'seniors tours'. Basically, interstate or local bus tours with a few overnight stays costing a few hundred dollars, as opposed to the thousands you'll need for a decent overseas tour.

These days you can organise your own travel itinerary and book all your flights and accommodation online, or you can choose to have a travel agent to do it all for you. You can travel around on your own or join an organised tour.

In places where I don't speak the language, I prefer to go with an organised tour, unless I know someone in country who is happy to show me around. I had a fun experience in Romania, where I had a friend who helped me buy a train ticket in Bucharest - a one-way ticket was all you could buy, mind you. When I needed to buy the ticket for the return leg, I encountered a middle-aged woman who didn't speak a word of English. There was a lot of laughter, as I negotiated using the only word in Romanian I knew - Bucuresti - so at least she knew where I wanted to go, and I found the word for Tuesday in the phrases in the Lonely Planet guide. At least with the money all I had to do was show her the notes.

One thing I can report from my travels is that most people are friendly. You won't get to meet them if you stay home.

When I go to Italy, I stay in apartments, which you can book online, and travel around on the trains on my own, because I speak the language. Another reason to study a foreign language or two. In fact, the last time I was in New York, I found myself speaking Italian in Penn Station, to two young travellers looking for the train to JFK airport, so you never know when a foreign language will come in handy.

Don't let anyone convince you that they speak English all over the world. They might in the hotels servicing tourists, but don't count on it, and if you want to get out and experience mixing with the locals, they'll appreciate the effort you made to learn a few words in their language.

If foreign languages aren't your thing that is no reason not to travel. There are plenty of English speaking countries to visit. Australia might be a long way from anywhere, except New Zealand, but it's a great place to visit, it's a lot bigger than most people think, and most of us are friendly.

Search for tours and travel destinations online or visit a travel agent and start planning.

## Catch up with friends

You might be living alone but you don't have to be a hermit. Just because your long-term relationship with your wife or partner is over, doesn't mean you're cut off from everybody else.

Make it a point to catch up with your friends for a meal or coffee, on a regular basis. If all your friends were 'her' friends, get out and join some groups so you can make new friends of your own. You're not the only lonely guy on the planet, or in your neighbourhood.

By joining groups or doing courses you can meet people with similar interests. All you have to do is be brave enough to ask questions, and remember, the easiest way to start a conversation is to encourage people to talk about themselves.

## Go to the game instead of sitting home with the box

Do you follow a football team, or any sports team, for that matter? Instead of watching the big game home alone, why not treat yourself, every now and then, by actually going to the game.

If you hate huge crowds, find a team in a local league or competition you can follow. That's another way you can meet people and, as I mentioned in the service chapter, local teams are always looking for supporters who can do more than simply attend games.

## STAYING CONNECTED

Some of us are introverts with a tendency to isolate ourselves. Others are extroverts and love nothing more than interacting with people. If you're with the extroverts, you can probably skip this - you already know how to stay connected.

But if you belong to the other group, or have tendencies in that direction, read on, because you probably need a gentle push to move you out of your comfort zone.

Most of us have a comfort zone, or group of behaviours, we prefer to stay with. A lot of us are resistant to change, and we withdraw into ourselves to cope with significant changes in our life situation. Losing your partner to death or divorce can be one of those devastating experiences, when all you want is to be left alone, to grieve. I understand that, but you can't stay there. That's a lonely, desolate place.

If you're feeling stuck in that desolate place, reach out to people who love you. If there is no one there for you to turn to, reach out for support through groups like Beyond Blue or Befrienders Worldwide. I don't want to be overly dramatic, but the statistics for suicide include a lot of guys who were not able to move on from the loss of their partner, and their subsequent loneliness. I'm here to remind you that you have other options, and some of them are as easy as picking up the phone to call a friend.

**Family**

By family, I'm talking about your children, your parents and your siblings, if you have any.

You're still the father of your children, your parents' son, and a brother, if you have siblings. These are the people who know you best, so continue your relationships with them.

Just because your living arrangements have changed, and you're now living on your own, doesn't mean you have to give up on family relationships.

If you're divorced, one thing you need to get clear is that the details of your separation are no-one else's business. Sometimes people with strong views can be judgmental. You're not a bad person because your relationship with your spouse or partner didn't work out. You know your family, so pick and choose who you relate to and who you want to share with.

In my opinion, it's good policy to speak kindly of your ex. Remember, things not working out the way you wanted doesn't magically make her a bitch. I understand if you need to give this one some time - but I encourage you to consider it.

Another thing to be aware of is good intentioned family members taking over the running of your life. They mean well, but it's your life, so keep hold of your power. It's okay to ask for help or advice but make your own decisions.

I'm part of a large extended family based around my birth family and in-laws. I come from a family of ten, so when we have family gatherings we often have quite a crowd.

I have different relationships with each of my siblings, and each of my in-laws. I even get along with my mother-in-law. I spend more time with some of them than with others. But we always have a good time when we are together as a group, even when we are attending a funeral.

One of the rowdiest gatherings we have each year is a cousins' dinner, with my wife's cousins and all our kids. This often starts in a restaurant and ends in one of our homes.

Families are great for giving support. I'm only on my own for those months of the year that make up the American school year, minus the one or two I spend in New York, but members of my extended family are always including me in things or asking me over for a meal.

Why am I sharing this? To remind you that whatever family you have, they can be a great source of support.

If you have children with young families of their own, remember that you're still a grandfather, and grandchildren can give you hours of enjoyment. Don't cut yourself off from their love and adoration. They will grow up soon enough.

## Friends

Beyond your family circle, you probably have a group of friends. These are the guys you grew up with, the guys you played sport with, the guys you work with, and the guys that see through all your bullshit.

They're also the guys you can talk things through with. Given the state of today's world, you're probably not the only one in your group who has experienced the end of a long-term relationship. Friends are there for each other. Sometimes they are there for you and other times you're there for them. So stay in touch. These are the guys who will remind you that life goes on, even after and through difficult experiences.

One of the challenges of coming out of a long-term relationship is maintaining friendships from that relationship. If you discover that those people you considered 'our friends' were actually 'her friends', it's time to step out and make some friends of your own.

You don't need lots of friends, but you do need to have a few guys with whom you can 'shoot the breeze' or share a bottle of red or go places. And guys, we are talking real people here. We are not talking Facebook friends.

If you have friends, go out and enjoy yourself. Take a course together, learn a foreign language and travel, join a service club, or exercise together. Go out on the town together. It's a lot more fun than doing it on your own.

If you need to refresh your friendship group, take a course in an adult or community-learning centre. Their courses are usually relatively inexpensive, fun and often involve a social dimension. Not only can you meet new people, you can experiment with new skills and enjoy yourself at the same time. You can attend courses for a day, a weekend or one night a week for weeks. You'll never know what the possibilities might be if you don't go exploring.

If you're religious, go check out the social groups at the local church - they might even have a men's group.

Remember, the pub isn't the only place people hang out.

## Neighbours

Often, we don't live next door to family and friends, but we do live next door to our neighbours.

When you live alone, it's a good idea to befriend at least some of your neighbours, especially if you're in poor health or don't have many family or other visitors.

Interacting with your neighbours is a way of making friends, but it's also a way of creating a network of people who look out for each other. Whether you like it or not, your neighbours notice your comings and goings and lack there of, just as you notice theirs. That could come in handy in a health emergency, and a neighbour is more likely to come straight away, if they know who you are when you call them for help.

Something else to consider is giving someone that you trust a key to your house or apartment, so that the neighbours, the police or ambulance crew, don't have to break the door in during an emergency.

**Pets**

If you find that you just don't like being home alone, consider getting yourself a pet. Walking the dog can be a great form of exercise but caring for a goldfish or two can also be rewarding.

Just remember that pets equal responsibility, and they cost money. There is a lot more to looking after a cat or dog than buying it food. Do some research before you commit yourself to picking up dog shit for the next ten to fifteen years. Maybe the goldfish option is not such a silly idea after-all.

**New relationships**

There are a lot of women out there living alone as well. Statistically, more women end up on their own following the death of their spouse than men. For some mysterious reason, they still seem to live longer than we do.

For every divorced man there is a divorced woman out there, somewhere. And, believe it or not, there are some women who have even chosen to stay single, and others who have put off entering into a long-term relationship because they haven't found the right guy, yet.

The interesting thing is that while many older single guys are looking for a new long-term partner, a lot of the girls are looking for something else. Some of this is driven by the differing expectations society has of men and women.

Men tend to get their freedom in their youth, and then settle down to become responsible, conservative citizens as they get older. Some get so conservative they turn into grumpy old men, but it seems even grumpy old men like to be cuddled.

Women on the other hand, often find themselves locked into the expectation of being a responsible wife and mother, until they move beyond childbearing age. This is when many women discover who they are, and walk away from existing relationships. Yes, despite all the Hollywood hype, it's the women who are instigating most divorces.

A woman released from a relationship, and all its expectations, by death or divorce, often finds herself free enough to be her own person for the first time in her life, even though she may be fifty, sixty or seventy. And, she's not likely to be looking for another relationship in a hurry. Many liberated women are not interested in looking after another man, especially a grumpy old one.

Sure, there will be some who want another long-term relationship, but don't count on meeting them where you hang out with the boys.

These days there are all sorts of relationships, and maybe you'll need to consider options other than the traditional one if you want a new partner.

If you want a new relationship, you'll need to get out of the house and go meet people. But don't rush into it. You need to give yourself time to recover from the end of your last relationship, before launching into another one with the first woman you meet. The statistics on rebound relationships aren't that encouraging either.

There are websites for finding people looking for new relationships. I can't recommend any simply because I haven't used any, but I'm sure our friend Google can help you with that, or ask your friends, especially those that have found themselves a new partner or love interest.

I know some wonderful couples that have come together after the ending of previous long-term relationships. Some of them have moved in together, while others spend time together but live in their own spaces.

A new relationship is a possibility, but you need to keep in mind that it's not the only possible or probable outcome. Many of us will end up on our own at the end of a long-term relationship, and that means embracing the reality of living alone.

**Resources**

**Support groups**

Befrienders Worldwide - www.befrienders.org

Beyond Blue - www.beyondblue.org.au

**Choosing a pet**

Wikihow - Choose a pet - www.wikihow.com/Choose-a-Pet

## BEFRIENDING YOURSELF

*There is a difference between loneliness (being isolated or cut off from others) and being alone (being on your own).*

For your entire life, you have been living with the best friend you could ever have - yourself. Unfortunately, most of us have lived our lives totally oblivious to that fact, and so, when we are on our own, we feel lonely. Some of us actually treat ourselves as the enemy.

It doesn't have to be that way.

One of the possible outcomes of living alone is finding out who you really are. I say one of the possible outcomes deliberately, because there are others, and you need to make a deliberate choice to embark on a journey of self-discovery.

I encourage you to make that choice, simply because the alternatives, like loneliness, depression and alcoholism, are not all that enjoyable. And suicide is final - you don't get to reconsider it after the fact, at least not in this dimension.

One of the first questions many people asked me when they found out I was living on my own was: 'Don't you feel lonely?'

My answer to that question is: 'No.'

I enjoy my own company and I'm always with myself, so I never feel lonely. Apparently, this is fairly common for people who meditate, because meditation allows you the opportunity to get to know yourself.

Being your own best friend is the easiest way of avoiding the loneliness trap when you live alone.

## Self-discovery

The external world is the focus of most of our attempts to understand the world and our place in it. It's true, there is a lot of interesting stuff in the world we can study, and we can keep ourselves busy for hours doing precisely that, as I have indicated in earlier chapters. In fact, you can hide there if you choose.

The journey of self-discovery, on the other hand, is an inner journey, which can be a very interesting, revealing, and surprising experience, as you encounter yourself along the way. You'll definitely discover that you are not who you currently think you are, if you undertake the trip.

Reluctant mystics, like me, have been on this pathway, off and on, for most of our lives, so I can introduce you to a few friends and techniques to help you undertake the journey of self-discovery, or as I often see it, the journey of self-recovery.

To make this journey, you need to turn your focus away from studying things outside yourself and start studying yourself. This journey is about noticing what's going on in your life and wondering why.

If you were divorced after ten or more years of marriage, instead of feeling angry, shocked or betrayed, recognise that as an event you could notice, and wonder why it happened. And, here's my first pointer: never wonder why anything happened to you but always wonder why it happened for you to notice. Ever wondered why some things appear again and again in your life? They keep happening until you notice whatever the hidden lesson is. That's why some guys end up being divorced multiple times.

What does it tell you about the person you have been presenting to the world, if the woman that you claim you love decided to leave you? I never said this was going to be either easy or comfortable, at least in the early days, but if you really want to befriend yourself, you have to be honest with yourself. That means shining a light on all those lies you tell yourself about yourself, and everybody else in your life, including the ones who have died.

This journey is not something you'll complete in an afternoon or by attending a weekend workshop. This journey requires commitment to ongoing exploration.

I suggest you start by learning to simply stop and check in with yourself, and, in my experience, the best way to achieve that is through meditation.

## Meditation

One of the first steps on the road to self-recovery is slowing down, and learning to sit and do nothing.

This is a major challenge for a lot of us. We've grown up in a society where we were encouraged to keep ourselves busy. In fact, a lot of us are actually addicted to activity, or our devices, and don't ever give ourselves any down time. Even when you're doing nothing in particular there is a voice in your head, that sounds a lot like your father's, mother's, some teacher's from your childhood, or, heaven forbid, your ex-wife's, telling you that you should be doing something.

That voice has been driving your decision making for as long as you can remember, and it will continue to do so until you tell it who's in charge.

Meditation is the first step to getting to that point.

When I first started looking into meditation, I was under the misperception that it was a religious activity. It can be, but it doesn't have to be.

The type of meditation I practice these days is called Mindfulness Meditation. It may have its roots in Buddhist practices, but you don't have to take on any beliefs to practise it. *Waking Up: Searching for Spirituality without Religion*, written by Sam Harris, a scientist, philosopher and famous skeptic, is an interesting read if you're interested in that perspective.

If you're particularly religious, you can follow a meditation practice aligned with your religion - they all have one - because all practices lead to the same place in the end.

The simplest form of meditation that I know is something you can try right now. Put the book down, sit comfortably in a chair, close your eyes, and just notice your breathing. Focus your attention on your breath and let any thoughts that come into your awareness float by, like clouds in the sky of your mind. If you realise you have chased a thought down a rabbit hole, simply bring your awareness back to your breathing. When you've had enough, slowly open your eyes and bring your attention back into the room.

When you first start meditating, you may find it difficult to sit still for even ten minutes at a time. Some people go to sleep well before ten minutes are up. Don't panic, and don't give up if that happens to you. It's fairly normal. If you snore, you'll wake yourself up, eventually - I did.

Start with ten minutes, and gradually increase the amount of time you meditate up to twenty or thirty minutes. Many teachers recommend meditating for twenty minutes two times a day.

You can set the timer on your smartphone to remind you when the time is up. A gentle chime works best.

Meditation needs to become an ongoing practice if you are seriously interested in befriending yourself.

There is a wealth of material, online and in bookstores, on meditation that you can tap into, and there are many meditation centres around the world where you can learn to meditate.

One of the books I find helpful is: *Wherever You Go There You Are* by Jon Kabat-Zinn.

**Journal work**

For some reason, journaling works best if you use a pen and paper, so get yourself a decent exercise book or visual diary, if you like to doodle and draw as well as write.

You can start journaling by asking yourself some questions and then simply writing down whatever answer comes up. The secret is not to think about it too much or to edit what you write. Just write - sometimes the answers really surprise you.

A few starter questions:

- What do I believe in?
- What could I live without?
- What can't I live without?

- What hurts am I holding on to?
- What do I want to do with my life?
- What are my special talents and qualities?
- How do I feel about (a specific event or person)?
- Why did (a specific event or person) show up in my life?

When you want to go a bit deeper, consider forgiving everyone in your life for all the hurts you have experienced.

Then consider forgiving yourself for all the hurts you have imagined.

Journal work can be challenging, so it might pay to work with some guidelines from others who have gone before us. A few books that I found useful are:

- *Your Ultimate Life Plan* by Jennifer Howard
- *Change Your Thoughts, Change Your Life* by Wayne Dyer
- *Real Happiness* by Paul Ferrini, and
- *Love is letting go of fear* by Jerry Jampolsky.

Another approach to journal work is to write out the story of your life. You don't have to share it with anyone but yourself. We're all carrying around the story of everything that has ever happened to us - the good, the bad, and the ugly things. Using a journal is one way of getting in touch with that story.

One resource for really getting in touch with your story is *Writing from the heart* by Nancy Aronie. I participated in one of her workshops in New York. Interestingly, most of the people doing the workshop were single women using writing as therapy to uncover their stories. It was an amazing experience.

Use this information to get started on journaling, but be aware that there is a lot more help available in the online library: just type 'journaling' into your search engine of choice.

One journaling activity I recommend is keeping a gratitude journal - a book in which you write down all the people and things in your life that you are grateful for. A list you can add to, and turn to on those days when you're feeling down.

**Resources**

**Books**

*Wherever You Go There You Are* by Jon Kabat-Zinn.

*Your Ultimate Life Plan* by Jennifer Howard.

*Change Your Thoughts, Change Your Life* by Wayne Dyer.

*Real Happiness* by Paul Ferrini.

*Love is letting go of fear* by Jerry Jampolsky.

*Writing from the heart* by Nancy Aronie.

**Journals with prompts to get you started**

Soulful Journals - www.soulfuljournals.com

# SUMMARY

On our journey together, we have covered the skills you need to look after yourself, including how to feed yourself, and nine strategies for maintaining your sanity while living alone.

Some of the skills require a little time to master but they are not that mysterious - once you start using them. There is no magic involved. You only need to have the confidence to start and the perseverance to keep going until you know you can do it.

If you treat cooking as a process, it's nowhere near as confusing as it first appears. Start with the simple stuff and leave the fancy recipes for later - if ever.

The first seven sanity saving strategies: reading, writing, learning a new skill, exercising, growing things, serving and having fun, are about finding constructive ways to occupy your time. Many of us are good at doing things, so I hope you found some things you can investigate or embrace as fulfilling pastimes. I also hope you'll have the courage to step out and challenge yourself to learn something new. It's a lot of fun - I've certainly learnt a lot about publishing and internet marketing since I decided to write a book, and it's been really interesting as well, especially for someone who was never ever going to be on Facebook or Twitter.

The importance of the last two sanity saving strategies: staying connected and befriending yourself, cannot be overstated. These are the two things that, in my humble opinion, will enable you to continue to enjoy life on your own.

There is a vast difference between being lonely and being alone. The choice to befriend yourself will help you appreciate that difference. It's a choice I encourage you to take.

The alternatives are nowhere near as enjoyable and all of them are detrimental to your sanity.

If you're looking for new friends or a new partner for the next phase of your life journey, embracing these strategies will put you in a much better position for going forward than staying home and feeling lonely.

My purpose in writing this book was to put a resource into your hands so you would have somewhere to start. I'm sure that there are many other things you could do other than what I have suggested, but sometimes you need a little nudge to get you started.

I hope I've given you that nudge.

If nothing else, I trust I have given you the information you need to look after yourself with confidence.

Enjoy the journey.


Peter Mulraney

Adelaide 2015

# A NOTE FROM PETER

If you found *Living Alone* useful, please consider writing a review or sharing the book's details on social media to help other readers find the book.

In addition to the Living Alone series, which is based on my personal experience of living on my own, I have written several other books you might enjoy reading.

You can find details about books and read my blog at **www.petermulraney.com,** where you can join my **Crime Readers Group** to download a free copy of *Deadly Sands* or subscribe to my monthly newsletter 'Insights from a crime writing mystic' and download a free copy of *A Question of Perspective* and be one of the first to know when my next book will be released.

# ALSO BY PETER MULRANEY

**Inspector West series**

After

The Holiday

Holy Death

Whistleblower

Twisted Justice

The East Park Syndicate

**Stella Bruno Investigates series**

The Identity Thief

A Gun of Many Parts

Bones in the Forest

A Deadly Game of Hangman

Taken

Fallout

The Identity Thief Collection

The Fallout Collection

**Novella**

The New Girlfriend

**Living Alone series**

After She's Gone

Cooking 4 One

Sanity Savers

Living Alone Journal

**Everyday Business Skills**

Everyday Project Management

Everyday Productivity

Everyday Money Management

**Writings of the Mystic**

Sharing the Journey: Reflections of a Reluctant Mystic

My Life is My Responsibility: Insights for Conscious Living

I Am Affirmations: The Power of Words

Beyond the Words: Reflections on I Am Affirmations

Mystical Journey: A Handbook for Modern Mystics

**Sharing the Journey Coloring Books**

Mandalas

Mandalas by 3

**Sharing the Journey Coloring Journals**

Sharing the Journey Coloring Journal

Discovery

Reflection

www.ingramcontent.com/pod-product-compliance
Lightning Source LLC
Chambersburg PA
CBHW071929290426
44110CB00013B/1529